TOGETHER
WE CAN DO MORE

The
Leon Williams
Story

by
Lynne Carrier

ISBN: 978-0-7442-3808-2

DEDICATION

This book is dedicated to Leon Williams, his wife, Margaret, and others in the Williams family, to his political colleagues, staff members, neighborhood councils, and all of the citizens who shared his vision and helped bring it to life. Together they did more.

I would like to see us go calling on the good example and upon
virtue itself with the purpose of inviting them back into our
conversations, our businesses, homes, and our lives, to reside in
those places as favored friends.

–Maya Angelou,
Wouldn't Take Nothing for My Journey Now

Table of Contents

FOREWORD

As I reflect on the many things that happened and changes that were made during my time as a public officeholder, I also think of the many people who were involved and made very important contributions to the achievements we made. Many of those were staff members. And, to all of my former staff members at the San Diego City Council, the San Diego County Board of Supervisors, and to the staff at MTDB/MTS on which board I served from its creation in 1976 to the end of 2005, and chaired for the last 12 years of my tenure, I profoundly thank you.

You were all, without exception, very fine human beings, devoted to the basic mission of government, and I honor and thank you. There were also many, many people throughout the City of San Diego and County of San Diego who were appreciative and continued to vote for me. Thank you all.

My hope is that this book will encourage people in decision-making positions, particularly in government positions, to be more considerate, less "I" oriented, and more inclusive of the ideas and opinions of fellow decision makers. This includes making decisions that will be sustainable in the long term and which are put in place for the benefit of all people.

Leon Williams

Leon and Margaret Williams (2014)

INTRODUCTION

Everyone Deserves a Place at the Table

How does an African American with humble beginnings in Oklahoma emerge as one of the most respected, well-liked politicians in San Diego, California? And how does a man known for his gentle, affable nature take on the rough and tumble of politics and emerge victorious – without creating enemies?

This is the story of one such man, Leon Lawson Williams, who mastered the art of persuasion and, in the process, set an example for anyone hoping to better the world. You only have to look around the landscape of San Diego County to see the signs of his legacy as a San Diego councilman and, later, as a San Diego County supervisor. The breathtaking downtown skyline, the budding commercial centers in previously ignored urban neighborhoods, the nationally admired trolley system, and the freeway call boxes for stranded motorists reflect the influence of this civic-minded public figure. Less obvious, but important nevertheless, are his contributions to services that improved lives, among them better prenatal care, more sensitive community policing, and help for desperately ill AIDs patients. These contributions often happened during years of controversy – times of racial and religious tensions – when his negotiating skills were tested to the limit. Yet he was able to rise above the controversy and put his personal feelings aside in order to pursue a greater good. He never lost sight of his mission, he believed there really could be a better world, and he performed his duties quietly, under the radar. He was among the leaders who went for results and did not angle for splashy headlines.

This is not only a biography about the life of Leon Williams. It also discusses how people can tap into the effective strategies that worked so well for him. Employing these strategies was not always easy. Anyone who has spent time around politics knows the public arena can be fractious and divisive. But Williams's simple approaches – sometimes as a vocal leader and sometimes behind the scenes – were powerful transformational tools. In the hands of a skillful political figure, these strategies were used to build consensus, deal with complex urban problems and, just as important, inspire a city to meet its bright potential.

That was especially true when Williams was first appointed to the San Diego Council in 1969, as San Diego's exploding population approached 700,000, making it the second largest city in California. A bigger city meant big-city problems – urban sprawl, overtaxed infrastructure, and social tensions.

Into this setting, Williams brought his personal brand of leadership. Those who knew him found a smart, likable man in search of common-sense solutions, a farmer's son with a strong appreciation for an urban quality of life, and an attentive listener who was equally skilled at advocating for what he felt was right.

His longtime council aide, William Jones, described his style as "disarming." Williams was able to reach past the rigid beliefs of others to get them to see his ideas in ways they had never before contemplated. Jones saw his former boss use this masterful form of communication time and time again, with top city officials, the police chief, bankers, whoever sat on the other side of his desk. "Once Leon gets everyone on a platform to discuss reason as the guiding principle, he wins," recalled Jones.[1]

When Williams was elected to the Board of Supervisors in 1982, he brought his effective approach with him, and it continued to serve him well. Brian Bilbray, a Republican and fellow county supervisor in the 1980s, described Williams's ability as "political judo." In 1986, Bilbray told the *Los Angeles Times*, "He takes momentum and doesn't stop it, but he turns it often back on itself. Leon has a way of getting you to do what you didn't want to do and getting you to like it."[2]

Williams, a Democrat, worked well with many of San Diego's Republicans. He did so with an abiding respect for those who saw the world differently. How could council or board members get things done if they made each other feel inferior or somehow less intelligent? He sensed instinctively that an elected official on the defensive was not going to be his ally. So, when his council colleagues dug in their heels and disagreed with him, he avoided confrontation.

"They just have a different point of view and a reason for that point of view," he said. "You need to solve a problem, and you both agree to that. There are advantages and disadvantages either way, and you talk about all those things. But not about the person. ... You never get personal. And you never assume a superior position. Never assume a position that I'm right and you're wrong. I never take that attitude."[3]

His second guiding principle focused on inclusiveness. Having grown up in a time of segregation, he had experienced the exclusionary impact of mindless, soul-crushing racism. These life lessons no doubt influenced his thinking as Williams succeeded in breaking the city's racial glass ceiling. He was the first black San

Diego city councilman, although with his usual modesty, he was quick to note that the first minority council member was Chinese-American Tom Hom. Williams also went on to become the first African American on the San Diego County Board of Supervisors, opening doors for other talented minorities.

His vision of inclusiveness went way beyond race and even beyond other equal rights categories, from gender and disability to sexual orientation. Everyone had to be included – the bus driver, the housewife, the immigrant, the professional, everybody.

He had an innate sense of what rightfully belonged to everyone. After he was appointed to the California Coastal Commission, for instance, he helped stop wealthy Northern California land owners from closing the beautiful coastline of 17-Mile Drive to outsiders. Maintaining access to a natural wonder on the Monterey Peninsula was a victory for the commission, the California Coastal Act, and the public. Williams took satisfaction in knowing that visitors from all over the world would continue to travel the highway along the rugged coast, where the iconic Lone Cypress stands like a sentinel overlooking the Pacific.[4]

Williams wove his beliefs into the day-to-day decisions of his public life with impressive results. Among his long list of achievements was the creation of the Centre City Development Corp., a key to transforming a dying inner city into a beautiful and vibrant downtown. As a board member and ultimately chairman of the Metropolitan Transit Development Board, he helped nurture a light rail system, and by 2014, the bright red trolleys were traversing 54 miles of track, with more lines in the works. He had the determination to bring one of those trolley lines into the heart of San Diego State University, a small city of more than 30,000 students and faculty with a notorious parking shortage.

Throughout his long and productive career, Williams earned respect for his ethics. He refused to succumb to the temptations that tainted – even ended – other political careers. In his first years on the City Council, he recalled that some people doing business with the city took him aside and offered him private deals–East County property or apartments at below-market prices. These offers sometimes came from interests seeking to curry favor with decision makers. He rejected every one of them. When it became clear that his answer would always be, "No, thank you," the land deal proposals faded away.

"Once I was in office, I made a commitment that I would never personally profit from my position," he said. "I was there to serve the public's interest."[5]

He avoided even the smallest ethical peccadillo. His unswerving adherence to that commitment became legend among his staff members.

Arlene Kirsch, his legislative and press aide at the county Board of Supervisors, told the story of a day in 1990 when Williams wanted to mail a personal letter. He asked if she had a stamp she could give him. When she offered him one, he hesitated, asking her, "Was this paid for by the county?" When she said yes, he refused to take it. The stamp may have cost a few cents, but they were pennies belonging to the taxpayers. And, therefore, that particular stamp never found its way onto his personal correspondence.[6]

Williams stands with his political consultant, Alan Ziegaus, who along with Michel Anderson, helped organize the dedication ceremony.

His accomplishments and high standards earned him numerous awards and accolades. One of the most moving was a plaque in his honor at the County Administration Center, unveiled after his retirement as a San Diego county supervisor. It read: "Be it proclaimed, by Chairwoman Dianne Jacob and the Board of Supervisors of the County of San Diego on this 24th day of February, 1995, that they do hereby thank and commend Leon L. Williams for his distinguished years of service to the people of San Diego County and for his contributions to the Board of Supervisors, recognizing his high ethical standards, compassion for the people he represented and his commitment to building a better San Diego."

Less visible to the public but also meaningful was an honor from fellow members of a fraternal society of high-achieving black professional men. Alpha Pi Boulé was the San Diego chapter of the first black Greek-letter fraternity, Sigma Pi Phi, also known as the Grand Boulé. It was a source of pride for Williams to be singled out for special recognition by his fellow archons, as fraternity members are called.[7]

There were many other honors. In 2007, for instance, San Diego State University bestowed an honorary doctorate on Williams and named a room at the university library in his honor.

Directions to the Leon Williams Room in the SDSU Library

Williams is not the type to let all that go to his head. Even at 92, he is the same solid citizen as ever. He lives with his wife, Margaret, in the Golden Hill house he has owned since 1947. It is a handsome Craftsman style home, immaculately maintained. Its original oak floors still gleam. Its windows and broad covered porch overlook his perfectly manicured yard.

In retirement, he is the poster guy for healthy living. He still goes to the gym and watches his diet. He has an engaging warmth, a sense of style reflected in his jaunty fedoras, a sharp mind, and a keen sense of humor, especially about the occasional foolishness of government. One of his favorite essays is C. Northcote Parkinson's little classic, "Parkinson's Law," poking fun at a bureaucracy that tends to expand even when the amount of work doesn't.

Williams is keenly aware, however, that not far from Golden Hill, San Diego's political leaders continue to wrestle at City Hall with the serious challenges of running a big city. He worries about the future. In his view, the deliberations of the council and other agency boards stand a better chance of succeeding if its members truly see themselves as equals. The same principles could apply at all levels of government, including the U.S. Congress, where the centrifugal forces of partisanship seem to spin each side farther from consensus.

In fact, these values, Williams believes, can benefit anyone trying to achieve goals through teamwork. They are not merely abstract ideals but skills that can be learned.

In a San Diego State University alumni newsletter, Williams, who graduated from SDSU with a bachelor's degree in psychology, offers this advice to college students:

> Learn to be a positive person and to see other people as your equals. Learn to see them as having brains and having a point of view that might be as good as yours, although different, and not be judgmental, but rather to be open-minded, hospitable and good-hearted. Be intelligent and keep your integrity and don't compromise for personal benefit. Do things you know are good for everybody.[8]

The quiet weapons of respect and civility proved effective for Leon Williams in his quest for a better city. They are also simple virtues, bridges to friendships and community appreciation. This book is dedicated to revealing the ways that one public figure learned and applied those principles during his successful lifetime.

The Leon Williams Room in the SDSU Library

Leon Williams's High School Yearbook photo (1941)

CHAPTER 1

The Road to Achievement

OKLAHOMA

Leon Williams began his life in rural East Central Oklahoma, far from the urban lifestyle he would one day embrace. He was born in the town of Weleetka, July 21, 1922, the first-born child of a hard-working farmer, Lloyd Ray Williams, and his wife, Effie Elvira Lott Williams. Soon after, his parents moved to a farm in Payne County.

He was the oldest child in what would become a large family. He eventually had 14 siblings—10 brothers and four sisters. As the eldest son in a growing family, he occupied a position of high expectations, and he was encouraged and permitted to learn early. One day, when he was 10, his father gave him a lesson on how to drive the tractor. He was so small that he had to crouch down to hit the pedals and hop up to steer. His mother thought he was too young. "My father would reply, jokingly, 'It's too late to teach him any younger.' Or he would simply say, 'Let's experiment.'"[1]

Leon's formal education was rudimentary. There was a rural segregated school with about 100 students a mile from his home. In his grammar school years, he walked to his classes. Eventually, the school obtained a school bus, making his life a lot easier. The students were taught reading, writing and math – the basics. Decades later, Williams revisited the school site, but all that was left was the building's front step and the foundation. "I remember thinking as a kid how big that step was, but now it seemed very small, not much of anything," he recalled. [2]

The Williams's farmland covered several acres in Payne County, between state Highway 33 and the Cimarron River. At the intersection of the main highway and the road to the family's single-story wooden farmhouse and barn were two businesses: a gas station owned by Doc Thornton, a friend of his father, and some tourist cabins – precursors of the motels built for travelers. But mostly there was little else but gently rolling country, constantly brushed by the prairie wind. The farm was a world of its own. The lifestyle of the family farm protected him from the social and economic convulsions of the larger world, even though the rural land imposed its own harsh exigencies.

His father raised a variety of crops, mainly cotton, corn, potatoes, and alfalfa. He did this without hired hands. Leon's uncle, Harvey Williams, had a farm nearby, and the two brothers would help each other with harvesting or any other activity needing more than one worker. His mother's kitchen garden produced beans, cabbage, and tomatoes, among other vegetables.

They farmed without pesticides, providing their growing family with a healthy diet of fresh food. They also kept chickens, pigs, horses, and cattle. His parents raised enough on the farm to be practically self-sufficient. They only needed to go to town to buy flour, sugar, shoes, clothing, and a few other basic provisions. Cotton and other crops not used by the family were sold at market, generating enough money to sustain the farm.

The work was hard, and Leon was expected to help his family with the milking and other farm chores. But he always remembered the quiet evenings of his childhood, the savory dinners his mother prepared, his exhausted father relaxing at the end of a busy day. His mother was an excellent cook, and whenever one of the pigs was slaughtered, she would prepare some of her pork specialties, like the delicious round sausages that young Leon loved to eat.

His parents were remarkably congenial, peaceful people. "They got along very well and never argued," he said. "They didn't look down on people, and they didn't look up to people. They just saw them as people."[3] Perhaps because of those personal traits, his father, Lloyd Ray Williams, became a successful man, a leader in his community, a singer in the church choir, and a Mason who got along with both African Americans and whites. His father had other talents, too. He was an artist skilled at shaping clay figures of people and animals. He owned an organ operated with a foot pedal, and he would fill the farmhouse with all kinds of music. "That was inspirational for me," said Williams. "They talked about musicians and composers. I knew about W.C. Handy before I could read."[4]

Both parents instilled good moral values and a sense of fairness and ethics in their children, even during the cynical days of the Depression. Neither of them drank, and Leon remembered how bootleggers in long coats came to the farm during the Prohibition years offering their wares—only to be turned away, disappointed.

The family found ways to break the tedium of rural life. Leon remembered that when he was a small child, his father bought a film projector. He would hang a white sheet on the wall, thread the celluloid through the newfangled contraption, and show a silent movie. The blurry, flickering image of a train seemed almost miraculous and stuck with Leon for the rest of his life. When Leon was older, he got his first radio, a crystal set. He replaced it later with an electric tabletop model. The family would gather around to listen to their favorite programs, from radio soap operas to the music of the Carter family. The dawn of electronic entertainment—the shared experience of mass media culture—had reached all the way to their farm, just as it had in the rest of America.

For the most part, their actual contact with the outside world took place within a few miles of their home. They enjoyed their occasional Sunday outings, although sometimes these could turn disastrous due to the fragile nature of the tires on his father's Model T Ford. On one of these outings, a tire blew. Stoically, his father jacked up the car and patched the hole in the tire, taking care not to let the inner tube bulge out and cause another blowout. He managed to finish the job, but his Sunday finery was a mess, smudged in dirt and sweat.

They never journeyed to the big Oklahoma cities, especially Tulsa, where one of the country's worst racial massacres erupted the year before Williams was born. Tulsa's prosperous black community, Greenwood, a neighborhood with 10,000 residents and a business district known as the black Wall Street, was all but destroyed in that incident. An estimated 300 of its African American residents died, and thousands were left without homes. The violence was sparked when a black man was acquitted of a charge of assaulting a white woman, and a group of African American men gathered around the released prisoner to protect him from a white lynch mob. Gunfire erupted, and when the Greenwood men retreated into their neighborhood to defend themselves, white men – many alleged to be Ku Klux Klan members – charged after them, torching Greenwood's homes and businesses and firing weapons.[5]

In spite of Tulsa's racial violence and its terrifying Ku Klux Klan resurgence, the Williams family was not afraid to run errands and shop at some of the small country towns in the area, where discrimination was less evident. "We could go into the stores without having to go in some side entrance," he said.[6]

Tiny details of these trips remained in Leon's memory. As a young child, Leon recalled his sense of wonder when he had his feet x-rayed at a store in Coyle, the closest town, to see if his new shoes were the right size. The transparency of the leather amazed him in an era when shoe x-rays were viewed as a helpful amenity rather than a radiation menace. He also remembered going to the oil town of Cushing for a tonsillectomy, probably not the most pleasant of his childhood memories except for the ice cream they gave him after the surgery.

The family occasionally visited Langston a few miles southwest along Highway 33. The town had special significance for African

Americans. The year after the 1889 Oklahoma land rush, Langston was established as one of several all-black settlements where migrants had come to escape the discrimination of the South. The town became home to Langston University, founded in 1897 as the Oklahoma Colored Agricultural and Normal University. At the time, it was the only black college west of the Mississippi.[7] It remains a public university, its brick buildings vividly standing out against the green of the campus and the fields beyond.

His grandfather on his father's side had been among the post-Civil War African Americans regarding the Oklahoma Territory as a "promised land" for anyone willing to work hard, regardless of race. According to family lore, his grandfather had been a strong leader with a dream of an independent life. He and his family hopped aboard a boxcar leased for African Americans and journeyed from Georgia to the town of Boley, Oklahoma.

At the turn of the 20th century, Boley was one of the most successful black communities in America. Its black residents owned or controlled virtually all of the town's institutions, from its bank to its utility company.

Despite the vigor of Oklahoma's black settlements, social conditions worsened for Oklahoma's African American population after 1907, when Oklahoma became a state. Newly empowered white leaders used their state's rights to impose Southern-style segregation laws.

In 1929 the stock market crash sent shock waves all the way from New York to Oklahoma. Then nature delivered another blow. In the 1930s, when Leon was still a child, Oklahomans suffered a long and severe drought. These larger, uncontrollable forces brought misery to Oklahoma's rural communities. The dry prairie winds turned once fertile fields into the Dust Bowl. The dust was so thick in some parts of Oklahoma that the skies turned black. Williams said he never saw the worst of the dust storms, but drought conditions and the depressed economy affected his father's farm. Eventually, thousands fled west in search of a better life. The Williams family joined the exodus.

CALIFORNIA BOUND

Williams recalled that when he was 14, he helped persuade his father to move the family to California. He knew exactly where they should go. His uncle, Claude Williams, who lived in Bakersfield, California, had been sending postcards with tantalizing pictures of waving palm trees and gaudy sunsets. If he didn't know it before, those images convinced him that his destiny lay far to the west of Oklahoma.

In 1936, his father sold off his farm equipment, his livestock, and most of his possessions. He rigged a canopy over the top of the flatbed of his 1929 Chevrolet truck. It seemed like a motorized version of a prairie schooner. The family piled aboard, and soon they were on Route 66, heading west.

During the journey, Leon pulled aside the canvas, watching the unfamiliar towns pass by. As they moved through one Texas town after dark, he spied a neon sign on a building depicting a martini glass and the flashing word "cocktails." "Dad, what's a cocktail?" he asked.

Economically, Bakersfield turned out to be a lot like Oklahoma. For both, oil and agriculture were the engines of growth. But there the similarities stopped. At the time the Williams family arrived, Bakersfield had a population of more than 26,000, which seemed like a huge metropolis after years of isolated rural life. It was flat, hot, and dusty, but it was also culturally and racially diverse and an important Central Valley center of commerce and trade.

Williams's father purchased 10 acres of farmland. He found work as a farm labor contractor, organizing crews to do field work. Later, he took a job as a gardener with the Kern County government. His mother was busy raising her still-growing family.

Leon Williams devoted his five years in Bakersfield to his studies. He attended Washington Junior High School and then went on to Kern County Union High School, a mega-campus with 5,000 students. It differed dramatically from his tiny, racially segregated Oklahoma grade school. In Bakersfield, blacks, Native Americans, Hispanics, Asians and whites went to the same classrooms, although all of the teachers were white. This diverse student body was generally well-behaved and respected authority. Williams said the school only had a single truant officer. The Bakersfield schools also offered a broad curriculum. In Kern County, he learned for the first time about the big and fascinating world beyond the borders of the United States.

He was an excellent scholar. He was also an intuitive thinker, constantly trying to figure out the reasons for what was happening around him. He never felt like he was part of the in-crowd. "In school, I always felt a bit different from other kids," Williams said. "I felt like they knew something that I didn't know or they would be doing stuff, and I wouldn't feel like I was part of it. I never thought I knew what was right. I always had some doubts."[8]

Later in life, his confidence grew. He came to realize that no one really had all the answers, and that people who thought they did tended to be trapped in their own rigid mindset. Having felt like an outsider in his youth, he spent his adult life helping others feel included – even the people who disagreed with him.

Leon Williams's Senior Portrait

A NEW LIFE IN SAN DIEGO

After graduating from high school, he had no trouble finding a job. Based on his outstanding results on a standardized employment test, he had three good offers – one from Lockheed, another in Vallejo, and a third at North Island Naval Air Station in Coronado, California, across the bay from downtown San Diego. At his father's urging, he accepted a job in production control of airplane parts at North Island.

In 1941, when he was 19, Williams left his family in Bakersfield and set out for his new life in San Diego. He was excited at the prospect of being on his own but had no idea what to expect. When his bus pulled into the downtown depot, he spotted the Pickwick Hotel nearby and thought he would spend the night there until he got his bearings. But Williams was about to have a rude introduction to segregated San Diego. The hotel clerk turned him away because he was black. Williams asked the clerk where he could go. He was told he could stay where blacks were allowed to stay. And where was that? "Oh, somewhere over there," the clerk replied, with a vague flutter of the hand. Fortunately, Williams had a high school friend in San Diego. He let Williams stay at his home until he could find a place of his own.

When Williams showed up for his job at North Island, he was assigned to be a painter's assistant, and he had to lobby to get the job he originally had accepted. Finally, he was transferred to production control for airplane parts, and he quickly settled into its blue-collar work environment.

A few months later, the Japanese attacked Pearl Harbor, plunging the country into World War II. The military gave him a chance to serve his country. It also introduced him to its institutionalized federal racism. Williams volunteered for the U.S. Air Corps but was turned away because of segregation rules. Shortly after, he was drafted into the Army, which could not afford the luxury of rejecting soldiers on the basis of color. The Army had a system in place for managing and separating soldiers of different races. Williams scored high on an Army test that qualified him for a psychological warfare position in Texas. But when the program discovered he was black, he was rejected. He wanted to go to Officer Training School, which was available to African American soldiers. Before he could apply, he was deployed to Australia and New Guinea. He had to wait until the end of the war to find his opportunities.

Post-World War II San Diego must have been a disappointment for African Americans who served their country and returned home. Public venues continued to bar patrons of color. When Williams returned to his civilian job at North Island, he still was not allowed into San Diego's white-only restaurants. Only one downtown restaurant, the Japanese-owned Sun Café, would serve him meals.

But the military had given him one important tool for advancement. The G.I. bill allowed him to leave his North Island job and attend San Diego State University as a full-time student. At the time, the university had about 5,000 students. Few of them were minorities. Williams could only recall about 10 African American students. "There were some Hispanics and Asians, too," he said. "But we were not allowed to participate in the student government or many of the real activities. We were kind of on the fringe of campus life."[9] Williams made the best of it. He joined the Toastmasters group, which attracted white students as well as minorities. He initiated the Intercultural Organization on campus. As a psychology major, he was allowed to join the Psychology Club, and he also took part in the university's Spanish Club and the French Club.

The Toastmasters Club at San Diego State College (1949)

He also participated in the Open Housing Movement, an early civil rights effort aimed at ending housing discrimination. "Segregation was pretty strong in those days," said Williams. "We'd go around and ask people to put stickers in their windows that said 'My neighbor can be anybody.'"[10]

The extent of his involvement made an impression. "The Black in Crimson and Black," a history of African Americans at San Diego State University, noted: "Considering the broad range of campus organizations he was involved in, and that he made it a habit to 'dress for success' wearing his signature double-breasted suit and tie, it was obvious Leon Lawson Williams (Class of '50) had big plans for the future."[11]

First row, left to right: Violet Allison, Pearl Cooper, Virginia Lester, Phyllis Holdway, Maria Luisa Hijar, Margaret Wilson, Ernestine Mendoza, Ann Ware. **Second row:** Al Henson, William Gerrish, Henry Schooley, Charles Rector, Ralph Frias, Howard Hopf, Jean Saint-Aude, Samuel Stuart. **Third row:** Paul Jacot, Ralph Castellanos, Robert Fitzpatrick, Leon L. Williams, Jack Walton, Harold Gadson, David Reyes-Guerra, Emilio Robledano.

The El Azteca Club at San Diego State College (1949)

After earning his degree at San Diego State, he was admitted to the Claremont College graduate school, where he hoped to earn a Ph.D. in psychology. But he changed his plan when the Korean War broke out and started looking for another job in San Diego. He was hired as a social worker with the county government. He was the first African American to hold that position. Within three years, he was promoted to supervising social worker. At the same time, he was pursuing a master's degree in public administration from San Diego State.

Leon Williams in the San Diego State Yearbook (1950)

Later, he moved into an entirely different county position when the Sheriff's Department hired him. There he rose to the position of principal administrative assistant to the sheriff. During his nine years with the Sheriff's Department, he had the opportunity to show his managerial skills. At the time he was hired, sheriff's deputies were based in downtown San Diego and would have to take their patrol cars vast distances to get to their beats in the outlying unincorporated areas. Williams established substations in East County and North County to cut their commuting time and save on gasoline expenses. He changed the existing system of having deputy sheriffs keep records at the main office. The deputies were freed for law enforcement activities when Williams helped establish positions for records clerks, court clerks, and a bailiff system.

In 1966, he left the Sheriff's Department to take a job as director of the San Diego's Neighborhood Youth Corps, a federally-funded War on Poverty program designed to help young people of all racial and ethnic backgrounds find jobs and develop their employment skills. The San Diego program, which operated under the control of the San Diego branch of the National Urban League, reached out to thousands, as far as Borrego Springs in the desert. Soon, the program was viewed as a national model and, Williams recalled, people from all over the country came to see how it functioned. A few months before his City Council appointment, he also took on a temporary position as executive director of San Diego's Urban League office.

The Neighborhood Youth Corps and Urban League positions helped raise Williams's visibility at the height of the civil rights movement, when Hispanics and blacks began to imagine the possibilities and believe they could emerge as an influential part of society.

Leon Williams dispensing advice at a meeting of the
Neighborhood Youth Corps (1969)

Leon Williams attends a City Council Meeting (1969)
Image used courtesy of KPBS

Chapter 2

Welcome to the City Council

In a 1969 KPBS documentary, newly appointed City Councilman Leon Williams took journalist Peter Kaye on a tour of San Diego – not to the beaches, the famous zoo, or the palm-filled parks familiar to tourists, but to the neighborhoods often ignored by the decision makers. This was a tour of Williams's Fourth District.

He represented most of San Diego's black and Hispanic neighborhoods, a fading downtown, and older communities left behind as the middle class rushed to the suburbs. His district was "in transition" – a euphemism for rapidly deteriorating.

Williams's televised tour of the district was an exercise in hope and despair. There was a stop at Sister Pee Wee's Soul Food on Imperial Avenue, where the owner would serve up fried chicken so delicious that her tiny eatery became a neighborhood sensation.

There were interviews with other black business owners along Imperial Avenue. They talked of forming a credit union and improving neighborhoods. And there was a visit to a San Ysidro teen post, where a battered piano and pool table offered recreation in an area that had little else for young people.

Williams also wanted to showcase the blight imposed on neighborhoods too powerless to stop it – the junkyards across from the bungalows of Barrio Logan, the illegal auto graveyard on a lot where, almost laughably, a sign warned against littering, and the freeways that had destroyed homes and isolated neighborhoods. He pointed out the "physical ugliness" imposed on residents who did not have the political influence to stop activities that devalued their homes.

As an African American, what did he plan to do to help these constituents? "I can put the ideas and the feelings and the sensibilities of black people and other minorities into the council," he said during the interview.[1] San Diegans previously excluded from the political process would have a voice.

Choosing Williams

Several weeks before his KPBS tour, Williams made local history by becoming the first African American to serve on the San Diego City Council. At the time, very few minorities held such important positions. One was an African American, Rev. George Walker Smith, a Republican who had been elected to the San Diego Unified School Board and who went on to found the civic organization, the Catfish Club. Another was Williams's predecessor, Tom Hom, an Asian American who was the first minority to serve on the City Council. Hom stepped down from the Fourth District City Council seat in 1968 after he was elected to the California State Assembly. Hom's departure from the council led to a search for a replacement who would reflect the diversity of the Fourth District.

Behind the scenes, several prominent African American leaders organized a community convention to support a candidate for the Fourth District seat. Activist Vernon Sukumu, who was a San Diego State University student at the time, argued initially for an open convention, with potential candidates getting an equal shot. But George Stevens, a Baptist preacher and community leader, wanted all the participants to get behind Williams. Stevens believed that Williams had the education and credentials to win the council's approval. If the community looked divided, or if support was scattered among several candidates, the council members might not choose an African American, and Stevens feared the opportunity might slip away.[2]

Williams recalled that Stevens and Judge Earl Gilliam visited his Neighborhood Youth Corps office and implored him to seek the council's appointment. When Williams stepped forward and made a presentation at the Fourth District's community convention, he won its resounding endorsement. He also won the support of a grassroots coalition of 23 groups called Black, Oriental, Mexican Brothers (BOMB).

The San Diego City Council considered 31 candidates and spent countless hours behind closed doors discussing their merits. Few were surprised when Leon Williams captured the appointment in January 1969.

He had admirable qualifications. At 46, he was a family man who had lived for years in the district he would represent. At the time, he and his wife, Dorothy, had three children – a daughter, Karen, 22, at San Francisco State University, a son, Leon Jr., 21, at his own alma mater, San Diego State University, and a daughter, Susan, 15, attending San Diego High School.

He had an impressive work record. His administrative skills were well-known and highly admired. Right before his council appointment, he had been offered a job as head of San Diego's Model Cities Department. It was an opportunity he had to turn down when he was tapped to serve on the City Council.

Also, Williams was no stranger to politics. He had been a volunteer for the electoral campaigns of Mayor Frank Curran. A Democrat, Curran was first elected to the San Diego City Council in 1955 and went on to serve as mayor from 1963 to 1971. Curran supported Williams's bid for the open council seat.

Williams was sworn into office January 7, 1969, and wasted no time in asserting his message of social inclusiveness. "I feel this is a very important occasion for the city, not necessarily because of the appointment of a minority person but because of the recognition that all of the people should participate in government," he said that day.[3]

On the council, the newcomer made a sunny first impression. He was handsome, with a neatly trimmed moustache. He was tall, just over six feet, with a runner's lean physique, and he was always well-dressed. Most striking of all was his ready smile and agreeable demeanor. Williams was a true believer in the non-violent strategies espoused by Martin Luther King, Jr. He spoke with the voice of calm and reason, reassuring San Diego's conservative establishment that he wasn't some fiery rabble rouser.

He sometimes worried that his aura of niceness might cause some people to think he was weak or naive. Nothing could have been further from the truth, according to those who knew him best.

"He had a steady, balanced approach to problem-solving, and he was relentless," said his longtime City Council aide William Jones.[4]

Williams had to walk a tightrope between those who wanted him to be more militant and his own beliefs on how to reach his goals. Screaming and calling people racists, he thought, would only alienate them and make it harder to get a favorable outcome. He wasn't really the strident type anyway. Decades later, he would reflect back on this philosophy of civility, confident that his approach had worked well for him. He said, "If you want to get results, you can't make enemies of all the people in power."[5]

It took at least five votes for the City Council to approve proposals. From this recognition he developed his political style – a style that seemed to come naturally. He would treat everyone with dignity, listen to their opinions, and find effective ways to argue his own case. The city had problems, and he would work with the mayor and the other council members to solve them. It was the best strategy for planting ideas and motivating colleagues to get results. Otherwise, he would be a lone voice of advocacy on the council.

Williams summarized it this way: "It takes power to do anything. I used to say, 'You can't undertake vast projects without vast power. And I had one-eighth vast power. And with that, you can't do much of anything.'"[6]

Leon Williams in his City Council office (1969)
Image used courtesy of KPBS

SMALL TOWN POLITICS, BIG CITY PROBLEMS

From the very beginning, Williams had his work cut out for
him. In 1969, the city's districts were still based on the number of
registered voters rather than population—a policy later invalidated
by the court and replaced with a system based on population. Since
low-income and minority communities tended to vote in lower
numbers, thousands of the non-voting constituents were ignored
when district boundaries had been drawn. As a result, the boundary
lines of the Fourth District wrapped around a huge chunk of San

Diego. It stretched from downtown through Southeastern San Diego, hopping over the incorporated cities of National City and Chula Vista, to include San Ysidro on the Mexican border. "I had more than 100,000 people in my district, and other members [of the council] had 65,000 to 70,000," said Williams.[7]

Serving all those constituents was a giant task, and Williams quickly got down to business. But he faced numerous obstacles. San Diego – the second largest city in California – treated its City Council as though it was the overseer of a small village. Council members had no funds to hire staff members for their individual districts.

The city staff prepared dozens of pages of background information on issues coming up on the council agenda, but there was little time – and no staff for the individual council members – to read and evaluate the materials. As an experienced administrator, the new councilman realized that he could not make good decisions without understanding the background information. "People were coming into the council wanting us to do more," recalled Williams. "There were all kinds of issues – zoning, land use, off-street parking, community conditions. Those were issues that the council should have known what they were doing. They should have anticipated the consequences of the communities they were creating or not creating or destroying. But the council was not that knowledgeable in those days."[8]

He wasn't sure whether some of his council colleagues wanted to know more. At times, they seemed to prefer the breezy social side of their job. Before California's open-meeting laws, council members would pile into a limo and go to lunch together. It never occurred to them that some might consider that back-room politicking. Occasionally, Third District City Councilman Henry Landt would invite his council colleagues, including Williams, to his home. These were purely social occasions.

But when it came down to the city's business, Williams didn't notice much enthusiasm. Sometimes the city staff's reports were treated like annoying piles of waste paper. After one council session, Councilman Landt looked over at Williams and asked, "Do you want to see what I do with all of this?" With a flourish, he shoved the thick pile of staff-prepared background material into the trash can by his seat.[9]

Williams found this casual attitude puzzling. The council's approvals and denials were helping shape the future of San Diego. The new councilman decided to strike out on his own to get the help he needed.

Kimball Moore, who became the city manager after Williams took office, loaned Williams some city staff members to work in his office. Mervyn Dymally, an African American state senator who later was elected California's lieutenant governor, sent him two assistants from a new intern program.

At the heart of this issue was the fact that the San Diego City Charter had no provision allowing City Council members to hire a staff. Only the heads of departments had that ability. Council members were provided a staff liaison who served all of them – and who answered to none of them individually.

The problem was finally solved when the city attorney ruled that the mayoral and City Council offices would be considered separate departments. Each would be able to hire its own staff. "Before that, the other council members didn't seem to care much whether they had a staff, but once they found out they could have a staff, most of them were happy about it," said Williams. [10]

Fixing the internal administration of his office was just one of his goals. To make progress in the Fourth District, Williams needed help from his constituents. To underscore the importance of community involvement, his stationery bore the slogan, "Together we can do more." One of his biggest challenges was to mobilize residents to support projects and proposals for improving their neighborhoods. By the end of his City Council tenure, almost every block had a Neighborhood Watch, and every neighborhood had a town council.

SURVIVING HARDSHIP

In the early days of his council career, Williams had to make
personal sacrifices to survive financially. This was because San Diego
council members faced a paradox: They had prestige, visibility, and
a horde of people wanting their time and attention. Yet they were
paid $5,000 year, less than a municipal trash collector received. The
popular view at the time was that San Diego had a city manager to
run the government. Council members simply attended meetings
and voted yes or no. But, in Williams's opinion, laissez-faire
government didn't work and threatened ruinous consequences for a
big, fast-growing city. San Diego needed strong political leadership,
carefully considered policies, and a vision. Williams began to pursue
those goals before the city government had a chance to catch up,
and it caused him hardship.

When he was first appointed to the council, he had kept his 40-
hour-a-week job at the Neighborhood Youth Corps in order to
support his family. He did his council work evenings and weekends.

By 1973, he had so much work at the City Council that he had
to give up the Neighborhood Youth Corps position. Henry Hill, the
chairman of San Diego's Urban League board, which contracted
with the Neighborhood Youth Corps, had issued an ultimatum.
Either Williams attended the Urban League's monthly meetings, or
he would lose his position at the Neighborhood Youth Corps. As it

turned out, the Urban League and City Council meetings overlapped, and Williams felt he had to attend the council meeting. True to his promise, Hill forced Williams out. The move drew protests from Williams's supporters. Vernon Sukumu found it particularly unfair, since Williams had turned San Diego's Neighborhood Youth Corps into a national model of excellence. Sukumu recalled that outspoken Baptist preacher George Stevens protested so vigorously and persistently that he lost his county government job.[11]

But Williams accepted the Urban League decision. He needed to stay focused on his mission at the city. He supplemented his city income when he could, teaching classes part-time at San Diego State University, for instance. It was a challenge to keep up with expenses. Since joining the City Council, he had divorced and remarried. His new wife, Martha, had given birth to a baby girl, Alisa, and he also had two step-children, Penny and Jeffery, to support. He looked for other ways to help make ends meet. He started a yogurt shop on the SDSU campus but soon sold it. A small business needed a lot of nurturing, and his City Council job continued to demand most of his time and attention.

In 1974, city voters approved a measure recognizing the mayor and council members as full-time employees.[12] That was a step in the right direction. Nevertheless, council salary increases were small and painfully slow. A salary commission was created to make recommendations on council pay raises, but the council still had to approve its own pay rate, which some council members found politically awkward. Williams, on the other hand, voted unapologetically for pay raises recommended by the salary commission. When a friend on the San Diego Unified School Board confided that he planned to vote against a proposed pay hike for board members – a modest increase that Williams saw as perfectly reasonable – Williams asked him, "Don't you think you're worth it?" The board member got the point and voted for the raise.[13]

After five years of hard work and long hours on the council, Williams saw his city salary rise from $5,000 to $12,000 a year. By 1976, council members were earning $17,000 annually. At the time Williams left the city in 1982 to take his seat on the county Board of Supervisors, his council salary had reached $21,000, still modest for such an important city job. (In 2015, a San Diego council member received a $75,386 base annual salary, not at a level with top city executives but at least above the poverty line.)[12] Once on the Board of Supervisors, which has its salaries increased according to an automatic formula, Williams saw his salary more than double to $45,000. It was enough to lift him out of the financial danger zone.

As a young man, Williams had dreamed sometimes of going into business and getting rich. Instead, his path led him into public service. At some point, he realized his career was never going to make him wealthy. Yet he had found his calling, transcended the lean years, and never looked back with regret. The civil rights leaders of the 1960s suffered worse conditions than he had. "When I thought of all those children marching in the South, being hit with hoses and dogs, my hardships didn't compare," he said.

MENTORING FUTURE LEADERS

Williams's staff – both at the City Council and later when he served on the Board of Supervisors – not only performed the day-to-day work, it evolved into a microcosm of the all-inclusive community he envisioned. Its members were talented men, women, blacks, Hispanics, Asians, and whites. After Williams's tenure, three of his African American staff members – William Jones, Wes Pratt, and Tony Young– were later elected to the Fourth District City Council seat. Williams's office had developed a new generation of community leaders.

Jacqueline Young, left. Leon Williams, center. Tony Young, right.

The first of the new leaders was William Jones, initially recruited at the age of 17 in late 1972. Before he met Williams, the high-achieving Morse High School student was headed for UCLA with a full academic Ralph Bunche scholarship. The star student was the Region 18 president of the California Association of Student Councils. In that capacity, he would fly to Sacramento to attend state Board of Education meetings and offer input as a student non-voting member. He had his own office at school and an administrative assistant to help with the paperwork. In his spare time, he played football, ran track, and worked at the Broadway Department Store on its youth council. He had a girlfriend and a green Ford Pinto.

One day, he received a job offer that would change his life. It came through the office of the principal, Frank Thornton, who sent a pink slip to fetch Jones from his American government class. San Diego City Councilman Leon Williams had called, looking for candidates to intern in his office. Thornton had recommended Jones, although the busy teenager didn't take the offer seriously. When he got home, he discovered that Thornton had called his mother, and she was excited about the possibility of her son interning with the councilman. As she donned her apron and proceeded to cook dinner, she explained to him that Leon Williams was one of the most important men in the community. "I told her, 'I don't know this Leon Williams, and I already have a job.'" But she insisted that, at the very least, her son should accept the interview.

Jones visited Williams's office once, then again, and soon he was spending as much time there as he could. He gave up track that spring in order to spend more time at City Hall. Williams, as it turned out, didn't fit any of his stereotypes of a local politician. "He was a futurist," he said. "He was progressive. He was modern. He wasn't boring."[14]

William Jones, ex-aide to Leon Williams.

Jones and his mentor would talk for hours, coming up with strategies for creating a more inclusive community environment. Much of his time at City Hall, though, focused on following up on citizens' complaints – for instance, fixing potholes and sidewalks or responding to flooding caused by sewer or water line breaks. It was not the high drama found on front pages, but it was a priority in Leon Williams's office. And, as Jones passed along the routing slips to the city manager's office, looking for solutions to an average citizen's problems, he realized that he could make a difference without really having much power.

At the same time, Williams couldn't believe his good fortune to wind up with such a capable young man on his staff. "William was so intelligent," recalled the former councilman. "He listened. He wasn't argumentative. He had thought about a lot of things."[15]

Williams convinced his young intern to give up his UCLA scholarship and go instead to the University of San Diego so he could continue to work part-time at City Hall. Williams told him, "You're going to get a bachelor's degree – a master's degree – in how the world really works."[16]

One important lesson involved communications. Jones had fancied himself a good writer, but when Williams gave him back an edited version of a letter, it was covered with correction marks. The councilman expressed himself in a certain style, with a sense of purpose and a certain emotional tenor, and Jones was expected to master that sort of writing.

Little by little, Williams was grooming Jones as a city decision-maker. Jones did not realize it at the time. In fact, he was making other plans. In 1982, while Jones was working on Williams's campaign for county supervisor, his boss dropped a bombshell. He wanted Jones to succeed him as Fourth District City Council seat.

Jones told him that he was applying for graduate school. "It was the only time I ever saw Leon get upset," recalled Jones. "He said, 'The trouble with you young people is that you want it all right now.'" [17]

It soon became clear that political machinery had been set in motion for Jones. Coming back from lunch one day, he ran into Mayor Pete Wilson. The mayor had spoken to Williams and assured him he would help Jones get appointed to the seat Williams was about to vacate. Jones agreed but told his boss he would serve only one four-year term, and he was true to his word. [18]

William Jones, Jones's mother Lillian, his father Robert, and Margaret and Leon Williams, right.

Jones was appointed to the vacant Fourth District seat in December 1982. He was elected to the City Council the following year, garnering about 66 percent of the citywide electoral vote November 8, 1983. History was repeating itself. Leon Williams and his city record had political coattails.

In 1987, when his term ended, Jones stepped down so that he could earn a master's degree in business administration at Harvard University and later pursue a career in the private sector. Williams's first City Council protégé was gone, but another of his aides, Wes Pratt, was waiting in the wings.

Years before coming to San Diego, Pratt decided he wanted a career in public service and even ran for the City Council in his hometown, Springfield, Missouri. He had lost that election and decided to move to San Diego and earn a law degree at the University of San Diego. His first love, though, remained government service. He worked briefly for California State Assemblyman Pete Chacon and, in 1982, he was hired by City Councilman Leon Williams. When Williams was elected to the Board of Supervisors, he brought Pratt with him, and as his executive assistant, Pratt helped Williams develop public programs. Pratt admired Williams's humanitarian spirit and eagerly memorized his way of working with his fellow county supervisors and constituents. "He set a standard for decorum," said Pratt. "He never said anything disparaging about anyone, and he was never vitriolic. He wanted to keep the discussion on a higher plane."[19]

In 1987, Williams encouraged Pratt to run for the Fourth District council seat that Jones was leaving, and Pratt jumped at the chance. But the opportunity almost slipped away before his campaign got off the ground. Pratt turned in 238 signatures on a candidate nominating petition, which he assumed would be more than enough to meet the 200 valid voters' signatures required by San Diego officials. To his dismay, the City Clerk informed him that only 179 of the signatures belonged to valid Fourth District voters and, therefore, his name would not appear on the ballot. At first blush, his situation looked hopeless. The San Diego City Clerk refused Pratt's request to reconsider. However, Williams urged Pratt to keep fighting a nominating petition that seemed more of a barrier to running for elective office than a legitimate requirement for candidates. Pratt took his case to court, where San Diego Superior Court Judge Richard Huffman ruled in his favor. He ruled that Pratt had "substantially complied" with the city's nominating petition requirement. Pratt's name was placed on the ballot, and he went on to win the election. [20]

In his four years on the City Council, he helped create the San Diego Housing Trust Fund, the city's Human Relations Commission, the Small Business Incubator Center, and the Urban

Corps of San Diego – the kinds of programs that Williams supported.

After leaving his council seat, Pratt returned to Springfield, Missouri, where he currently works as the Missouri State University Equal Opportunity Officer and Director of Institutional Equity and Compliance. Yet he has not forgotten the lessons – both practical and idealistic – that he and other staff members learned from Williams. "Leon was able to inspire young people and could identify young talent who were committed to something greater than themselves," Pratt said. "So all of us... felt and believed that we were making a difference to whomever we served in whatever capacity."[21]

*Wes Pratt with Leon Williams at Williams's
County Supervisor Swearing-in Ceremony*

*Leon Williams being interviewed by KPBS in front
of a San Diego Community Relations Office (1969)
Image used courtesy of KPBS*

CHAPTER 3

Righting Civil Wrongs

Williams took office during a time when the civil rights tensions of the 1960s hung heavily in the air. Memories still lingered of the anger-fueled rioting in Watts and other African American inner-city communities across America, and battle lines had been drawn at the highest levels of law enforcement. FBI Director J. Edgar Hoover was targeting black militants. A few days before Williams was sworn in, the *San Diego Union* quoted Hoover as saying that black extremist groups were "a potential threat to the internal security of the nation."[1] Although San Diego had not experienced the massive rioting that burned in Los Angeles, the fear seemed to drift with the ashes all the way down to San Diego City Hall. Williams could sense the mistrust in the council chambers. Even the most benign groups were viewed with suspicion.

Leon Williams in a Council meeting (1969)
Image used courtesy of KPBS

On one occasion, the City Council deliberated on whether to cut off city funding to the Citizens Interracial Committee. More than 50 people – among them the CIC board president, Donna Salk, Dr. Jonas Salk's first wife – attended the meeting in support of continued funding for the organization. During the meeting, Williams was called away from the council chambers to return a phone call from Congressman Lionel Van Deerlin. When Williams exited to the outer corridor, he noticed that the phone he planned to use was already off the hook. A police officer posted next to it warned him to leave the line open. Then Williams looked around and saw a phalanx of police officers, almost elbow to elbow, lining the corridors that surround the council chamber. Williams was dumbfounded. This was a human relations group of eminent citizens, with a board of trustees including Bill Kolender, a future San Diego police chief, George Stevens, a future San Diego city councilman, and Carlos LeGerrette, a well-known Mexican American leader. Its executive director was Dr. Carrol Waymon, a respected psychologist, civil rights leader, author, and lecturer.[2] The proceedings inside the City Council chamber were calm despite the group's disappointment about the prospect of losing city funding. Williams approached Walter Hahn, then the city manager, and asked him, "What are these peace officers doing here?" Hahn whispered back, "Just in case."[3]

This extreme style of policing was something he had never encountered in his youth. Williams did not recall seeing a single police officer during his childhood in rural Oklahoma, and when he moved to Bakersfield, California, only rarely did he spot a motorcycle cop on the way to a high school football game. In San Diego, police officers seemed to be a hovering presence, and when there were protests, they showed up in riot gear.

"The first time I was stopped by a police officer I was on the City Council," said Williams. One night, when he was driving in Clairemont, a mostly white neighborhood, a police officer pulled him over on the pretext that one of his taillights was out. But the taillight wasn't out, and, Williams said, when the officer realized he had stopped a councilman, he drove off. On another occasion, a police officer stopped him while he was driving a city vehicle sometimes used by the police chief. The worst incident came in broad daylight in Balboa Park, where he had parked his VW van on an interior access road off Sixth Avenue. He had opened the side of the van and was reading over his City Council docket. "A police officer came up to me with his gun drawn. He said, 'What are you doing here?' I said, 'Put that damn thing down.'" Once the first encounter had cooled a bit, the officer explained that someone in the apartments across the street from the park had phoned police about a black man engaging in suspicious activities. Williams doubted his story. "I reported all those things to the city manager and the police chief," he said. "They did look into these incidents, but the officers lied, and I didn't want to make it a big issue."[4]

And if patrol officers had stopped a black councilman – seemingly for no reason – he wondered what these officers were doing to other African American motorists. He had heard troubling reports that San Diego officers routinely hassled young African Americans and Latinos. He witnessed incidents that made him cringe. Police officers would perch on a hill on the north side of

Ocean View Park, with their guns pointed down in the direction of kids playing below.

Once on the City Council, Williams often drove around late at night, trying to determine how bad the situation had become. Complaints about police behavior poured into his council office. He assigned his intern, William Jones, to sift through the citizens' complaints. While some were found to be false claims, many others were credible enough to pass on to the city manager's office for further investigation. Williams felt he had to speak out. On the council, he scolded police officials. "You're acting like storm troopers. You're supposed to be peace officers," he told them on more than one occasion.[5]

He knew, of course, that improving police behavior was going to take more than a stern rebuke. Even before his days on the council, Williams had advocated policies he believed would help develop better peace officers. For instance, when he was the top administrative aide at the Sheriff's Department, he pushed for higher educational requirements for sergeants and lieutenants. These standards, he believed, would help develop the skills and sensibilities of the department's supervisors.

On the San Diego City Council, he resolved to do what he could to reduce the tension between the police and the minority communities they patrolled. But it was not an easy period to improve police practices. There was too much unrest and distrust. He sensed that misgivings about law enforcement rumbled just below the surface of the Fourth District, threatening to surface and ignite protests at any time. Aggressive police tactics only made things worse.

DEATH AND THE PANTHERS

During his first year as a council member, Williams received a visit from San Diego Police Chief O.J. Roed and an FBI agent. They came with alarming news. They told him that the local Black Panther Party had a contract on his life. Black Panthers might be waiting in the shadows to ambush him when he pulled up to his house. They offered Williams a police escort. The councilman tried to hide his consternation. He wondered whether his two visitors realized that Kenny Denman, a San Diego Black Panther organizer, was one of Williams's supporters. Denman was actively working on Williams's election campaign and, unless he was engaging in some kind of nefarious conspiracy, which Williams doubted, the councilman was inclined to dismiss the law enforcers' warning. Williams said, "I thought they were telling me these things to try to discredit some of the African American activists. They wanted to separate me from them. What kind of credibility would I have if I drove around my own neighborhood with a police escort? "[6]

Meanwhile, Williams grew increasingly concerned about the violence erupting between the local Black Panthers and the US organization, another group of African American activists. "We heard the two organizations were headed for all-out war," said Williams.[7]

The confrontations in Southeastern San Diego began escalating early in 1969. In April that year, members of the two rival groups traded angry words and blows in Southcrest Park. The same day, US members disrupted a Black Panthers educational meeting.

The conflicts grew deadly. A Black Panther, John Savage, 21, was shot and killed May 23, 1969, at 30th Street and Imperial Avenue, not far from the Panthers' San Diego office. In August of the same year, a second Black Panther, Sylvester Bell, 34, was murdered in Williams's council district. Bell had been selling Black Panther mimeographed newspapers at Otto Square, a small shopping center on National Avenue. Williams went to the crime scene. It was all too vivid. "I saw his blood on the street," he recalled.

Both deaths were linked to US organization members. The jury deadlocked on murder charges against Savage's killer, who later pleaded guilty to a lesser charge of manslaughter. In the Bell case, which had resulted from a violent face-off between members of the two rival groups, one man linked to the US group was convicted of murder. Two others were found guilty of being accessories to murder.

Shortly after Bell was shot, rising tensions between the two groups prompted Williams to team up with Earl Gilliam, another respected African American pioneer, to attempt peace talks. At the time Gilliam was a Municipal Court judge, who later served as a judge on the county's Superior Court and then on the federal bench.

Williams and Gilliam visited the Black Panther office on Imperial Avenue. In the wake of the Black Panther murders, the building looked like an armed camp. Two men with shotguns guarded the entrance. The councilman and the judge explained that they wanted to discuss recent events with one of the group's leaders. The guards pointed their guns away from the visitors and let them climb a tall, narrow staircase to the second floor office. There they met Elmer "Geronimo" Pratt, the leader of the Black Panthers' Southern California chapter. Williams noticed a gun conspicuously displayed on a table next to Pratt. This was perhaps understandable in light of the recent San Diego deaths and the fact that Pratt had ascended to power after the two founders of the Southern California chapter – Bunchy Huggins and Bunchy Carter – were gunned down by rivals in Los Angeles. Nevertheless, Williams remembered Geronimo as pleasant and polite, a willing listener.

"We told him that violence between African American groups would only weaken their cause," said Williams.[8]

Williams and Gilliam also visited the US organization. The San Diego chapter was headed by local activist Vernon Sukumu. Again, the councilman and the judge pleaded for calm. "We warned him that they were falling into a trap," said Williams.[9]

Years later, Sukumu remembered that visit. He wondered how the rivalry between the black activist groups had escalated so quickly and what more could have been done to head off the murders. There had been a time when the US group had admired the bold militancy of the Black Panthers. "The Panthers and US should have talked at the first sign of hostility," said Sukumu.[10] Instead, bad feelings festered and ended in violence.

For Sukumu, it was particularly painful to learn that Sylvester Bell – a man he knew, a man who left behind a family – had been gunned down by a member of his own group. He hadn't been surprised that confrontations with Panthers caused US members to "talk bad" to their rivals. And in one case, they had grabbed some Panther newspapers and destroyed them. But that was a far cry from murder.

Williams said that during his meetings with the rival groups, both leaders complained that the rival group published leaflets and flyers with insulting messages and derogatory cartoons, causing tempers to flare. In the wake of Bell's shooting, the *San Diego Union* reported that one Panther newspaper described the US national leader as a pig and called local US members sissies who were part of the "power structure."[11]

It would be years before Williams learned about the origin of the inflammatory messages. In 1975 the United States Senate Select Committee to Study Governmental Operations with Respect to Intelligence Activities, chaired by U.S. Senator Frank Church, issued a series of reports, including one on the FBI's Cointelpro, short for Counterintelligence Program. It helped shed light on the earlier dispute between the Panthers and the US groups. "Neil Good (his staff assistant) brought me the Church report and showed me that the FBI had delivered those insulting messages and cartoons to the Black Panthers and the US group," said Williams. "The groups had nothing to do with them."[12]

For Williams, the revelations in the Church report came as a surprise. At the time he and Gilliam reached out to the Black Panthers and US group, they had no idea that the FBI was using deceitful tactics to ratchet up hostility between the two groups. The extent of the FBI's involvement in fostering violence in San Diego was discussed in Curtis J. Austin's 2006 book, *Up Against the Wall: Violence in the Making and Unmaking of the Black Panthers*. Austin, a scholar of the black power movement, described an FBI that was not at all ashamed of its actions. He wrote that after Black Panther Sylvester Bell was killed, the San Diego FBI field office sent a memo to its headquarters stating that "in view of the recent killing of BPP member Sylvester Bell, a new cartoon is being considered in the hopes that it will assist in the continuance of the rift between the BPP and US."[13] Those trouble-making opportunities evaporated by the end of Williams's first year on the council. In November 1969, the San Diego police raided the Panthers' headquarters, citing outstanding traffic warrants. Six Black Panthers were arrested. Shortly after, the group's leaders in Los Angeles decided to shut down their San Diego branch.[14]

The disclosures in the Church report reminded Williams of the importance of standing united for civil rights, sticking with peaceful protests, and not allowing outside influences to divide African American organizations. The corrosive impact of jealousy, betrayal, internal disputes, and sometimes unbridled violence threatened to sabotage their efforts. It took lives senselessly. It made them look like common gangs rather than representatives of a noble political movement. It made them more vulnerable to infiltration. And it could render their leaders useless to their cause (neutralized, as the FBI put it).

Certainly that was the case with Geronimo Pratt. The year after he met with Williams and Gilliam, Pratt was charged with murdering a woman and attempting to murder her husband as part of a 1968 robbery on a tennis court in Santa Monica. He was convicted, even though defense attorney Johnnie Cochran (the same Johnnie Cochran who later represented O.J. Simpson in his murder trial) argued that Pratt had been attending a Black Panthers meeting in Northern California at the time of the incident. Pratt – a Vietnam veteran with two bronze stars, a silver star, and two purple hearts – spent nearly 27 years in prison, including eight years in solitary confinement, before his conviction was finally overturned. He was released in 1997 and later received $4.5 million in a federal lawsuit settlement for false imprisonment. By that time, the Black Panther Party was history.

POLICING FOR THE PEOPLE

Although Williams did not know at the time how closely the San Diego police had been working with the FBI on its counterintelligence tactics, he did feel certain that the department had major problems in dealing with the public, especially African Americans. On the council, he supported local police reforms, from better recruiting and training for officers to providing more educational opportunities. He met on occasion with the city manager and the police chief to advocate less aggressive police behavior. Above all, he wanted to see policies that encouraged patrol officers to get out of their cars and acquaint themselves with people in their daily lives and not just in response to emergencies. When he worked at the Sheriff's Department, he noted that sheriff's deputies often moved to the outlying communities they patrolled, becoming neighbors as well as law enforcers. This was the essence of community policing. "They're supposed to help maintain peace in the community, not drive around like some kind of suppressor," observed Williams. "We even had some of them out there on bicycles."[15]

And, during his tenure on the City Council, Williams saw gradual improvements at the San Diego Police Department. The city made visible changes to soften the image of the police. In 1969, the police changed from black-and-white cars to white police vehicles. White cars were thought to be less intimidating and more in line with goals of community policing. In the 1970s, the community policing strategy began to show results. It even produced some surprisingly positive encounters for the officers themselves. Williams recalled receiving a letter from a white police sergeant who recounted how he gotten out of his car at a liquor store on Euclid Avenue. "He was describing how pleasant it was that he had done that," said Williams. "He got out of his car and actually talked to people as human beings."[16]

Williams also supported policies that would help recruit and train more officers of color. There had been a few black officers when he came to the council, Williams recalled. But they seemed demoralized. "I met with them several times to try to make them feel better," said Williams. "They were not well-treated. Some said they were called the 'N word.' They felt like they were not given full police power."[17]

Williams also pushed for good police leadership. One person in particular stood out as a good choice for police chief, Bill Kolender, and Williams lobbied the city manager to promote him. He had met Kolender when he was a sergeant and Williams was heading the Neighborhood Youth Corps. Kolender – Williams described him as a "good-hearted guy" – was named San Diego police chief in 1975. Both the city manager and the new police chief worked to recruit officers knowledgeable and sensitive to the needs of a diverse city, where residents spoke different languages and practiced different customs. Kolender was praised for his positive community image, his administrative skills, and his efforts to recruit officers who reflected the city's demographics.

Yet in 1985, three years after Williams had moved to the county Board of Supervisors, the city's police department experienced one of those flashpoints that periodically reopens old wounds and widens the racial divide. It happened when a white officer stopped a young African American male, Sagon Penn, on an Encanto street and asked for identification. Something went awry, and a terrific struggle ensued. With the officer on top of him, Penn managed to grab the officer's gun, shooting and injuring him, and then running over him as Penn fled the scene. He fatally shot a second officer and injured a woman who was riding along with police that night. Community tensions rose, with many in the minority neighborhood convinced the entire incident was due to over-policing and abuse of power. Near the end of the first trial, Williams said authorities warned him the verdict might provoke a community backlash.

Penn's defense attorney, Milton Silverman, argued successfully that Penn was defending himself from excessive force and fired on the officers only because he was fighting for his life. Penn was acquitted of murder charges. The jury deadlocked on an accusation of manslaughter, and a second trial acquitted him of manslaughter and attempted murder charges. For many who were critical of police behavior, justice had been served. The expected public protests never materialized. But police officers were stunned, and their bitterness lingered for years.

After the trials, Penn lived an unhappy life, plagued with legal scrapes, mostly related to domestic abuse and restraining order violations. He spent two years in prison for a probation violation. He spiraled into depression. When Penn committed suicide in

2002, Bill Farrar, president of the San Diego Police Officers Association, was quoted in the *San Diego Union-Tribune* as saying, "We don't have him out there creating problems now. As far as the Police Officers Association is concerned, the world is better off without him."[18]

In the years following the Sagon Penn incident, city officials tried to make changes to restore confidence in the police department. They created a citizens advisory panel, which made recommendations. Most notably, a Citizens Review Board on Police Practices was approved by San Diego voters in 1988. Some of the changes, however, seemed to undo previous efforts to soften the police image. The police department decided to paint its patrol cars black and white, more authoritative looking than the white vehicles police had driven since Williams's first year on the council.[19] Uniforms went from tan to the standard official-looking dark blue.

Yet Williams viewed these changes as symbolic setbacks that did not derail the larger goals of community policing - the need to build trust and personal relationships in the minority neighborhoods, the need to see all San Diegans, regardless of race, as people deserving of their protection and service, and the need for training and education so that each succeeding generation of officers would inherit a sound set of policies. Insensitive, indiscriminate use of force could only lead to more social unrest.

"There will be trouble as long as some people see the mission of the police as controlling the 'other people,'" Williams concluded. "We spend a lot of money on police officers, restrictions, and 'Thou shalt not.' I think people could do much better if they understood why society needs to be peaceful and how your safety is improved if your neighbor is not afraid of you."[20]

Campaign Pamphlet (1969)

CHAPTER 4

Connecting with Voters

Williams barely had time to warm his City Council seat before he faced another challenge. He needed to run for election in September 1969, only months after starting his new position.

This was no easy feat considering the heavy work demands of his regular council duties and his day job at the Neighborhood Youth Corps. Running a campaign was an entirely separate job. Still, Williams wasn't exactly a political neophyte. As a teenager, he volunteered for a Bakersfield city councilman supported by his father. Later, he had been a volunteer in the San Diego City Council campaigns of Frank Curran and Floyd Morrow. He had learned the fundamentals of campaigning, with its need to raise the profile of the candidate and connect with the voters.

At the time he ran for his own seat, the San Diego City Council candidates faced two electoral challenges. First, they competed in primary elections in their districts. The top two finishers then ran in a citywide general election. Williams's district was huge but had a history of light voter turnout. He needed a good message and a small army of volunteers to garner votes.

Luckily for Williams, the coalition of supporters that helped him win the appointment was ready to help him win the election. While these volunteers may not have had a lot of money to contribute to his campaign, they had the hopeful effervescence that marked the civil rights era. There was something in the air that helped generate enthusiasm for Williams's campaign. At last, an African American had ascended to a powerful position on the council, and they were not going to see him defeated after a few months in office. Among the volunteers was a wide assortment of community groups active in the Council's Fourth District, including a member of the San Diego chapter of the Black Panthers. Another community activist, Joe Vinson, staffed the campaign office set up at 3175 National Avenue.

Besides his grassroots supporters, Williams had the backing of some of the city's heaviest hitters. In his corner were powerful Democrats like Clinton McKinnon, a newspaper publisher and former congressman. McKinnon began publishing the daily newspaper, the *San Diego Journal,* during World War II. After the war, he sold the paper and ran for Congress, serving two terms in the U.S. House of Representatives.

In 1969, McKinnon took over as Williams's first campaign chairman. Labor leader R. R. Richardson became the co-chair. His treasurer was civic-minded James F. Mulvaney, an attorney who worked for C. Arnholt Smith's Westgate Corporation and was responsible for bringing the Pacific Coast League's San Diego Padres into Major League Baseball in 1969, the year of the election. Also helping the candidate was Williams's friend and adviser Mervyn Dymally; the helpful state senator was later elected California's first African American lieutenant governor. Other prominent supporters included San Diego Mayor Frank Curran, downtown businessman George Scott of Walker-Scott Department Stores, and financier C. Arnholt Smith.

The campaign worked to put together a winning strategy. Williams and his supporters wanted to capitalize on his City Council incumbency, but they could not call for his re-election since he had been appointed. They opted to use the word "retain," which suggested he was already on the job and deserved to be kept on the council. With that in mind, Williams's election organization was named the Committee to Retain Leon Williams on the City Council.

The candidate wanted voters to view him as accessible, willing to listen and respond to their concerns. His campaign motto, repeated over and over, was "He cares about people!"

A campaign brochure laid out his vision for San Diego's future – a philosophy that would serve to guide Williams's actions as an elected official:

> My biggest concern is bringing sensitivity to city government... making our city government responsible for human concerns and desires rather than just dollars and cents matters. As we enter the 1970s, San Diego must be concerned with the human problems of its 700,000 people if we are to escape the disaster and decay of this nation's larger and older cities.
>
> There must be a human element to our physical planning process. The city is where people live. It can be ugly and abrasive with air pollution, noise and traffic congestion, and frictions, or it can be exciting and inspiring to the people who live it.[1]

Williams beat both of his opponents in the Fourth District primary held September 16, 1969. His only serious challenge came from a fellow Democrat, Art Akers. Williams recalled that "it surprised me because he had supported me before for City

Council."[2] Williams easily outdistanced the two other candidates, taking 73 percent of the primary vote.

There was no time to celebrate the victory. The citywide election loomed less than three weeks away. Being the first African American councilman had been an advantage when he ran in the primary, limited to the district. But some of his advisors suggested that he downplay his race in the general election, in which a white majority could decide the outcome. Williams recalled that some of his supporters actually thought he should not show his face at all. Williams scoffed at the idea. He set up coffees and campaign events throughout the city, including Rancho Bernardo, a well-to-do, mostly white suburb far from Williams's Fourth District neighborhoods. In the citywide election held November 4, Williams captured 63,392 votes, or more than 60 percent. Akers finished a distant second, with about 40 percent.[3]

Under City Charter rules, Williams did not get a full four-year term after his first election. He had to run in the fall elections of 1971. Akers challenged him again, with similar results. Williams took more than 60 percent of the Fourth District primary and 105,826 votes, nearly 61 percent, in the November 2 citywide election.[4] This time, he won a full four-year term.

Meanwhile, a court ruling led to a significant change in the boundaries of Williams's council district before the 1975 election. It would reshape the city's political landscape – particularly for African Americans and Latinos – far into the future.

In April 1971, Superior Court Judge Hugo Fisher ruled that the city had to redraw its council district boundaries based on population rather the number of registered voters, the method San Diego had been using. The city's existing process was unconstitutional because it violated the one-person-one-vote principle, according to the ruling.[5]

The eight council districts were supposed to have roughly the same number of people. By counting only registered voters, the city had left Williams with a sprawling district and thousands more constituents than other council members. Although Fisher's ruling was good news for Williams – it would shrink the size of his district and make it easier to stay abreast of its needs – it stirred resistance in some quarters. An editorial in the conservative *San Diego Union* criticized the court ruling, calling it "disturbing," and came down hard on non-voters, saying that "it is difficult to understand the reasoning which holds that council representation would be more equitable if the negligent citizens are given unsolicited attention."[6]

San Diego City Attorney John Witt appealed Fisher's reapportionment ruling, a move that mainly succeeded in creating a long delay. When the city lost its appeal, Witt responded by challenging the Appellate Court ruling at the California Supreme

Court. Community groups were outraged. Daniel Muñoz, president of the Spanish Speaking Political Association, accused Witt of racial bias, saying that Witt was using "every means at his disposal to attempt to deny a sizable segment of the population of San Diego their right to equal representation at City Hall."[7] The California Supreme Court rejected the city's appeal in October 1972, forcing the city to comply.

It was more than 18 months after Fisher's order that City Clerk Ed Nielsen presented the City Council with four reapportionment maps for consideration. Williams did not like any of them. Each one split up black neighborhoods into different council districts, diluting their voting strength.

Besides the desire to preserve a viable district for African Americans, Williams wanted a reapportionment that would cluster Latino neighborhoods into a separate district. That would give them a better chance of electing Latinos to at least one seat on the City Council. Williams was sensitive to the paucity of elected Latino leaders at the time. In 1970, Pete Chacon became the first San Diego Latino to win election to the California state assembly. "I promised him that I would never run against him," said Williams.[8]

Williams teamed up with Eighth District Councilman Jim Bates to insist on a reapportionment plan more acceptable to African American and Latino community groups. In the next round, the city clerk came up with a map that kept most of the African American population in the Fourth District and added Paradise Hills, an ethnically diverse community. The Eighth District was dramatically reconfigured, picking up several Latino communities, including San Ysidro and Barrio Logan, which had been within Williams's previous district boundaries. Under the maps Williams and Bates favored, African Americans and Latinos would have a strong voice on the City Council in two separate districts for many decades.

Only one member of the City Council, Henry Landt, objected. He complained bitterly and publicly that the new redistricting plan amounted to racial segregation.[9] Williams saw it from a different perspective. Segregation had little to do with lines on a map. It was a real world phenomenon caused by a variety of factors from racism and poverty to white flight. And the proximity of the affected communities was only an advantage if they could join forces to make their voices heard. Drawing boundaries that placed them in a single district gave them better political options, an opportunity to choose their own leadership and seek solutions to their common problems. "In those days, from my point of view, they [other city officials] didn't see any problem in our communities," said Williams. "They didn't see underrepresentation of minorities, or lack of justice or inadequate facilities."[10] Stronger representation was what the communities needed – and what they got.

On January 24, 1973, the deadline set by Judge Fisher, the City Council approved the redistricting plan unanimously. Landt, still unhappy, ultimately voted with the others.[11] The reapportioned districts set the stage for a Latino, Jess Haro, to take over the Eighth District council seat in 1975. He was the first of several Latinos to sit on the City Council in the years that followed.

The new boundaries let Williams continue to represent African American neighborhoods in Southeastern San Diego, a Fourth District constituency that already knew him and supported him.

In 1975, five candidates ran against Williams in the Fourth District primary, but the results were almost the same as in the previous elections. Williams won more than 53 percent of the Fourth District primary votes, with Jesse Albritten coming in second and earning a spot in the citywide runoff election. The incumbent councilman went on to capture 61 percent of the citywide electoral vote November 4, 1975. Four years later, he was re-elected again, taking 60 percent of the citywide vote.

Seemingly invincible in his City Council seat, Williams opted for change, running successfully for the San Diego County Board of Supervisors in June 1982. Although he was well-known in the community by then, he needed help with his campaign. Home builder Tawfiq Khoury stepped in to become his campaign manager and chief fundraiser. Williams took the supervisorial position vacated by Jim Bates, who was elected to the U.S. House of Representatives that year.

Williams spent 12 years as a county supervisor, winning re-election to four-year terms in 1986 and 1990. He decided to retire in 1994. He and his wife, Margaret, looked forward to some free time. Williams rarely took vacation leave. Said Williams, "I was already 70 years old, and I had been working all my life. My notion was to get out and enjoy some of that deferred gratification."[12]

As it turned out, retiring from elected office did not mean leaving public life. Williams continued to serve another decade as the appointed board chairman of Metropolitan Transit.

Leon Williams, with his wife, Margaret, after his county retirement

Pete Wilson and Leon Williams

Chapter 5

Land Use Struggles

Williams thrived on building a City Council consensus. But occasionally he felt so strongly about an issue that even if he failed to get a majority, he voted his conscience. This happened during votes on huge new suburban subdivisions, especially along Interstate 15. The city couldn't keep up with the needs of these neighborhoods. Yet the City Council kept approving one project after another.

In his first months on the council, he voted against a North City residential development project, Mira Mesa, which was going to bring thousands of new homes to an area between Peñasquitos Canyon and Miramar Naval Air Station. Williams saw this pattern of development as a suburban disaster in the making. He argued that massive construction was premature, since the building site lacked city services. Not only did the other council members approve the project, Williams said, but a staff member from the City Attorney's office tried to stop Williams from opposing it. He told the councilman that the preliminary map had been approved before he was appointed to the council and that the vote on the final map was merely a formality. "He said, 'You can't vote against this,'" recalled Williams. "I said, 'Just watch me.'"[1]

Inevitably, the building boom caught up with City Hall. Mira Mesa home buyers began organizing protests. "The council chambers filled up a couple of times with people saying they had no parks, no fire stations, no libraries, nothing," Williams said.[2]

Besides Mira Mesa, other dense subdivisions were sprouting up and down the Interstate 15 corridor – Rancho Bernardo, Rancho Peñasquitos, and Scripps Ranch. Right before Williams's eyes, the city seemed to be splitting along the seam of Interstate 8. As the city's population mushroomed, people and resources moved north of I-8 to new communities. The trend left many of that the older urban neighborhoods south of I-8 with a lower tax base, diminished services, and schools with plummeting enrollment. There was no end in sight.

By 1970, San Diego had passed San Francisco as the second largest city in the state, with more new residents arriving every day. Growth was spinning out of control, seemingly flinging more residents into the city's peripheries. Suburban construction so thoroughly absorbed the building industry that San Diego City Manager Walter Hahn complained the city could not find contractors to bid on its approved projects downtown, among them the $4.5 million city Operations Building and the reconstruction of the Food and Beverage Building in Balboa Park.[3]

Besides newcomers, residents from San Diego's older, urbanized neighborhoods were moving in droves to these new suburbs. Williams was especially disturbed by the racial overtones involved in this migration. When he took office, there were white residents in Southeastern San Diego. But he saw that they were moving out, and minorities were replacing them, from Valencia Park and Emerald Hills to Encanto, Chollas, and Rolando. In one case, he said, the Irvin J. Kahn Co., which was developing dense tracts in the North City, encouraged white residents to leave Emerald Hills – and relocate to its University City development — by pointing out that blacks were moving into their Southeastern San Diego neighborhood. Williams couldn't stand the block-busting marketing practices that fostered racial segregation. And he saw that this population trend was threatening the city with added social and financial burdens. It concentrated the poor in older neighborhoods, where residents' wishes for better city and educational services often went unheard. Meanwhile, city officials scrambled to find the millions they needed to build new infrastructure for the fast-growing crop of subdivisions going up north of I-8.

Williams knew this pattern couldn't continue without breaking the city's bank. The city could no longer afford to build roads, parks, libraries and other services for the new subdivisions and properly maintain the roads and infrastructure of the existing communities. But when push came to shove, a disproportionate amount of tax revenue was going to the recently built neighborhoods. "It was almost like stealing," said Williams. "The property taxes from the older neighborhoods were going to the [new] communities, and the established neighborhoods were left with hardly anything."[4]

In 1970, state, federal and local officials began taking steps that somewhat slowed the scorching pace of suburban construction. That year, the federal government created the U.S. Environmental Protection Agency and the California Environmental Quality Act of 1970 went into effect, requiring developers to submit environmental impact reports.

The same year, Williams worked with the city manager on a policy that would moderate the impact of development on city services. Policy 600-10 required that before the council approved a subdivision proposal, the developer had to show that access roads and other public services would be available for a development at the time they were needed.[5] Williams remembered that it was hard to get a council majority for Policy 600-10. There were still council members who thought the city should not regulate development at all. When the council finally approved the policy in May 1970, it contained a bombshell. Subdivision approval would only happen when the affected school districts certified that they could handle the new students generated by the development. "We gave the schools the power to say no," recalled Williams. [6]

Suddenly, suburban developers who built homes and expected the city to pay for new access roads, fire stations, sewer hook-ups, and other services faced the possibility that their construction could be stopped in its tracks.

In November 1971, the City Council rejected a subdivision plan submitted by the builder Leadership Housing Services Inc. for its Miramar Ranch project in the Scripps Ranch area. San Diego Unified School District had stated it was unable to accommodate the students who would live in the neighborhood. The developer sued, saying the city had no authority to halt the project because of a lack of classrooms. Williams wasn't sympathetic. The *San Diego Union* quoted him as saying that although he didn't expect the builder to solve citywide problems, "when the developer chooses to build where there are no schools, then he has created a problem in his area."[7]

By the start of 1972, Mayor Wilson had taken office and quickly waded into the controversy. He was determined to lead a charge against uncontrolled, disorderly growth. The City Council even debated a possible temporary building ban for Mira Mesa, which brought howls of protest and legal threats from developers. Although the mayor and council backed away from a construction moratorium, the city continued taking actions to slow the pace of suburban sprawl. In the coming years, the city enacted a growth management plan designed to phase in development more gradually. Developers had to come up with impact fees to help cover the cost of installing access roads and public services. Later, in 1987, state law was changed to let school districts impose their own impact fees on developers. These laws and policies signaled the end of suburbia's free ride.

But the city continued to grow north of Interstate 8, and Williams continued to show his displeasure. One of the most telling examples was when Mayor Wilson persuaded shopping mall developer Ernest Hahn to commit to building the Horton Plaza shopping center downtown. If Hahn made that commitment, the developer would then receive the city's approval to build another of his huge malls, University Towne Center, in University City. Hahn agreed to Horton Plaza, and in May 1975, a majority of the City Council approved the proposed construction of University Towne

Center. Williams and Maureen O'Connor were the only City Council members to vote against it. [8] As much as Williams supported downtown redevelopment, he didn't feel the city should cave in to developers in order to get them to build in the Centre City. In his opinion, granting permission for another growth-inducing suburban mall wasn't worth the price. "Suburban sprawl was a negative," he recalled. "I didn't think you should give in to something bad in order to get another thing that is good."[9]

TOUGH LOVE FOR THE FOURTH DISTRICT

During the early 1970s, Williams also set his sights on building mechanisms to reverse the decline of older neighborhoods. He started by recommending a massive review of zoning in his entire district. As a result, there were numerous zoning changes. Some areas would wind up with increased housing density, others with a lower number of units that could be built on property. It was difficult and messy. These actions angered some people, including a few of Leon Williams's friends. He told them he wanted to create compatible zoning that would lead to more sensible use of land. In the end, good land use practices would better protect property owners' investments, he assured them.

As a councilman, Williams worked to make sure the established urban neighborhoods got a fair share of the city's tax dollars for everything from sidewalks and lighting to library branches and police substations. His former council assistant, William Jones, now an urban developer, said the overall impact of Williams's work is that San Diego's infrastructure in older neighborhoods is superior to the conditions found in other cities. Without that investment in infrastructure, Jones said, the resurgence of neighborhoods like Hillcrest, Normal Heights, Golden Hill, City Heights, among others, would have been far more difficult, if not impossible. "It doesn't necessarily get you a banner or building named in your honor, but Leon believed that it was critically important," said Jones.[10]

Williams needed grassroots support for these ventures and sought ways to engage citizens in their community development. He began organizing neighborhood councils that could discuss the needs of their areas and, if necessary, pack the City Council chambers on meeting day to lobby for anything from repairing roads to paving alleys.   To be effective, he needed them to fight for their own communities.

He was living proof that with patience and determination a citizen could prevail in the face of land use injustice. In 1947, he was able to purchase his home in Golden Hill, despite restrictions on the deed prohibiting blacks from owning the property. He had the help of a sympathetic real estate agent and Bank of America, which gave him the loan. At the time, African Americans were generally prohibited from buying homes north of Market Street.

Also, before he was elected to the City Council, he had stopped the California Department of Transportation from building a Highway 94 off-ramp that would have landed close to his front yard and destroyed some of his neighbors' homes. He went to the Caltrans offices and protested. "They tried to tell me it would be a convenience to have the ramp so close, but I didn't agree," he said. "It wouldn't have any benefit."[11] In the end, Caltrans decided to build the 30th Street exit ramp farther away from his property.

Once on the council, he would rely on that same gritty determination to help organize neighborhoods and build a better city. He was convinced that working at the local political level was the best place to fight prejudicial land use policies. And from his local office, he could raise the decibels on problems bothering people in his Fourth District.

One of the frequent neighborhood complaints he heard as a councilman focused on the liquor stores in their midst and the patrons who drank and loitered in front of them. With the vocal support of these neighbors, Williams persuaded a council majority to pass ordinances prohibiting loitering or locating liquor stores near schools, churches or day care centers. "Before, liquor store owners were a little afraid to tell people they couldn't loiter," said

Williams. "But after we passed the ordinance, they could point to a sign saying the city would not allow them to loiter, and the police could enforce it."[12] Other communities – and eventually the state – took note and passed similar ordinances. San Diego had led the way on a thorny neighborhood issue.

Not all issues fell into place so easily. During Williams's first year on the council, Interstate 805 was under construction near the border, taking out San Ysidro houses in its path and dividing the community. Williams held night meetings to give unhappy San Ysidro residents and businesses a chance to sound off. But many seemed demoralized. "They saw the city government almost as an oppressor," recalled Williams. "They felt like they didn't have any rights. They just had to tolerate whatever the city did. That was their kind of psychology."[13]

Some of those feelings were justified, said Williams. The city's bureaucracy, he felt, did little to reach out to the community. Nevertheless, Williams urged the aggrieved residents to speak up. He told them, "You are citizens. You have rights, but you've got to address your rights. You've got to stand up for them. You've got to stand up for them in a civil way. You've got to let people know, articulate what your feelings and what your desires are."[14]

FIGHTING MANO A MANO IN THE BARRIO

Meanwhile, in Barrio Logan, the councilman was trying to deal with the opposite situation. The social activism surrounding land use was so intense that it threatened to bubble over into a dangerous confrontation with police. Williams understood the nature of the barrio's frustrations. Before World War II, he had lived in Barrio Logan on the fringe of downtown. At that time, he recalled, it was a vibrant Mexican American neighborhood with a prime location on the bay. It had a bank, a five-and-dime store, and other commercial establishments. After the war, progress exacted a heavy toll. In 1963, the Interstate 5 freeway was built straight through the heart of the barrio, taking out scores of homes. The shipyards and docks dominated the bayfront. The city decided the barrio would become an industrial zone. The change seemed to come overnight. Residents woke up to find out they had junkyards – *yonkes* as they called them — for neighbors.

The final straw came after the construction of the San Diego-Coronado Bridge brought traffic ramps and huge concrete pillars into the barrio. Barrio activists – a mix of college students, residents, business people, and Brown Berets, among others — asked the city to help them create a park on the land beneath the towering new bridge. They mistakenly thought they had a deal. State officials, who had acquired the land in August 1969, had other ideas. The small brick building that the state constructed under the bridge's elevated onramp was intended for the California Highway Patrol. On April 22, 1970, construction crews showed up to build a parking lot for CHP patrol cars. Emotions boiled over as residents and students stormed the site and formed human chains to block the construction work. They were not going to move until they were sure that the land was given to the city for Barrio Logan's new park. They had a vision for it and even a name – Chicano Park.

Coronado Bridge under construction.
Image used courtesy of the San Diego History Center

At first, Williams had not favored a park under a bridge. He wanted Barrio Logan to have "a real park like other communities had." Once he saw their determination and understood that the park was as much symbolic as recreational, he supported them. Their passion was conveyed when on April 24, 1970, he called a

meeting with some of the Chicano Park protest leaders at the
Neighborhood House, a community center that since has become a
health clinic. "The only way to take that park away is to wade
through our blood," warned one activist at a public meeting.[15]

Chicano Park protesters (1970)
Image used courtesy of the San Diego History Center

At the time, Williams assured them that the state had agreed to
suspend construction while state and city officials negotiated with
neighborhood representatives. Privately he was worried. The
councilman went to Sacramento to meet with California Secretary
of Business and Transportation James Hall and Captain Vincent J.
Herz of the California Highway Patrol. He was distressed to learn

that they were not particularly interested in reaching agreement with the barrio residents. In fact, they wanted San Diego police officers to forcibly remove the protesters. If the city wouldn't do it, they could always use their CHP officers to get the job done. Williams searched for words that might cause them to reconsider.

He recalled, "I told them, 'You're going to go there and kill people and shoot people in that community and then have your headquarters right under the ramp onto the bridge?' I think they were suspicious because I was implying that they were going to make enemies of these people and then they were going to have a building right under the bridge. Anybody can throw anything onto that building. They got scared. It softened their line a little bit, I think."[16]

By the time Williams had returned to San Diego, there was tangible evidence that his words had sunk in. He noticed that a protective fence had been installed over the disputed structure.

On May 4, 1970, Williams attended a neighborhood meeting at Lowell Elementary School. He told a crowd of about 200 neighborhood residents that they would, indeed, get their park. The *San Diego Union* reported that some in the audience were skeptical. But their councilman had told them the truth.

If the residents of Barrio Logan had crystal balls that night, they might have been surprised to see their future. In the end, the state would surrender to the desires of the neighborhood, backed by the city of San Diego. The city would receive the state's land under the bridge in exchange for giving up some city-owned property in Mission Valley for a CHP station. The brick building at the center of the confrontation would become a community center instead of a CHP command station. The city would develop a park of nearly eight acres for the people. Mexican American artists would turn Chicano Park's cold gray bridge supports and columns into jewel-like works of art, their colorful murals depicting Mexican and Chicano history. The people would get another park on the waterfront. Housing developers would come to the barrio and build attractive and affordable rental units. The Mercado project in the shadow of the bridge would bring them a Gonzalez Northgate supermarket and restaurants. The residents of Barrio Logan may not have realized it in 1970, but they had won a victory beyond their imagining.

THE BATTLE OF HIGHWAY 252

The saga of California Highway 252 spawned another fierce land use struggle between freeway advocates and a diverse neighborhood that happened to be in the way.

Williams viewed the controversial highway plan as the kind of public project that mindlessly tore through African American communities not only in San Diego but across the nation. This highway plan seemed especially unnecessary, although for its own reasons, neighboring National City fought to get it built.

The proposed state highway had been planned as a 1.8-mile connector linking Interstates 805 on the east and 5 and 15 on the west. When Williams took office, work was beginning, and by 1972, the California Transportation Department had demolished 280 homes in the 66-acre highway corridor. Williams protested, and the project was eventually halted. He started making his move after Jerry Brown, a Democrat, was elected California governor in 1975 and responded to the neighborhood's concerns. Three years later, the San Diego City Council rescinded its agreement with the state, and two years after that, the California Transportation Commission officially dropped Highway 252 from its highway plan.

The view of the redeveloped Highway 252 corridor and its parkland.

It still could have turned out badly. For years, the highway corridor lay abandoned, like an ugly, litter-strewn gash across the Southcrest neighborhood. But this was destined to be a story with a happy ending. The Southeast Economic Development Corp.—created at Williams's recommendation – began redeveloping the highway corridor, bringing the neighborhood a sorely needed supermarket, new housing, parks, and a commercial center. After Williams moved to the county Board of Supervisors, Williams's City Council successor and former staff member, William Jones, picked up the gauntlet for highway corridor redevelopment. The neighborhood declared victory, and blight was transformed into homes and amenities.

The view of the San Diego ferry landing from the Coronado ferry landing (1969)
Image used courtesy of Dan Soderberg Photography.

Leon Williams, looking over Downtown San Diego from Coronado Island (2015)
Photo courtesy of Carlos LeGerrette.

Chapter 6

Healing the Heart of San Diego

Williams is holding a faded black and white photo depicting a desolate urban landscape, with blocks and blocks of low buildings. This was downtown San Diego on the skids, showing signs of the decay and abandonment that afflicted downtown neighborhoods across America. He had snapped the photo in 1969, shortly after he took office as a San Diego city councilman. It was the view from his 10th floor office window.

This earlier San Diego bore little resemblance to the one that would emerge in the 21st century – a city with thousands of luxury condos, stores, shops and hotel rooms, a bustling and rejuvenated historic district with dozens of restaurants and nightclubs, a huge convention center stretching for blocks along San Diego Bay, a downtown major league baseball stadium, and a new central library with a gleaming contemporary dome.

By comparison, the Centre City of 1969 looked forlorn, shabby. An exodus was in full swing, with downtown businesses migrating to Mission Valley and the suburbs to the north. After dark, a visitor often would have to look for signs of life by going south of Broadway, where seedy massage parlors, peep shows, X-rated theaters, and tattoo shops continued luring sailors, just as they had for many decades in this Navy town.

View of the Community Concourse and Civic Theater (1966)
Image used courtesy of the San Diego History Center

Williams, who represented downtown when he first came into office, thought this city by the bay should remain the heart of San Diego's urban metropolis, even if its pulse was weakening. During the 20th century, it had been a bustling urban center, and during World War II, military activities brought an abundance of revenue into the heart of the city. He thought there was every reason to restore its former vitality.

From his council office, Williams looked for signs of hope – and there were a few. Beyond the tired buildings south of Broadway, he could see the last span of the San Diego-Coronado Bridge being lifted into place. The bridge, curving like a blue ribbon across the bay, would soon connect downtown to North Island Naval Air Station and the tourist mecca of Coronado, with its wide beaches and the historic Hotel Del Coronado.

Across the street from his City Hall office, a stylish 242-room luxury hotel, the Westgate, was under construction. Developed by financier C. Arnholt Smith, it was decorated lavishly with expensive antiques, Persian rugs, and crystal chandeliers. When it opened in 1970, the Westgate blocked the city view from Williams' office window – the view depicted in the photo he had taken the previous year. But he didn't mind. The Westgate was a glamorous urban showplace, a statement of confidence in Centre City.

As a downtown supporter, Williams could also take some comfort that the Centre City remained a hub for county, state, and city government offices, as well as county and federal courthouses. San Diego City College on the east side of downtown was on the verge of undergoing a major expansion in the 1970s. On the bay, the military had a presence. The old Naval Supply Depot, with a view of North Island Naval Air Station across the bay, continued to function at the foot of Broadway.

He wished in retrospect that the city fathers had carried out an earlier plan that would have built a mall of government buildings along Cedar Street. The idea was to have a row of government buildings on each side of the street, connecting Balboa Park to the County Administration Center on the bay. The idea faded with time, especially in the 1960s when city leaders decided to relocate San Diego City Hall from the waterfront to the center of downtown. Williams thought it had been a mistake to remove San Diego's municipal offices from the beautiful Depression-era County Administration Center and install its functions in a 13-story City Hall blocks away on C Street. "It was much easier to coordinate when the city and the county were together," he said.[1]

But the decision to relocate city buildings to the central part of downtown had been made years before his tenure on the council. The new complex, completed in 1964, included the City

Administration Building (City Hall), a Community Concourse named for a previous mayor, Charles Dail, a civic theater, a convention center, and a parking structure. It was a significant urban renewal project, although its backers had struggled to find money to build it. City officials decided against putting a bond measure on the ballot to help cover the $15 million construction cost. Voters had defeated earlier bond measures for downtown civic projects on Cedar Street, one in 1947 and the other in 1956. The latter measure, which would have paid for construction of a convention hall and civic theater on Cedar, received a majority of the votes but not the two-thirds needed for approval.[2]

The city wound up raising construction funds for the City Hall complex by selling $3.5 million of publicly owned land and borrowing $8.4 million from the municipal retirement fund. A private committee raised another $1.6 million from wealthy donors to get the project started. It was clear the city would need better mechanisms to finance the rebirth of downtown.[3]

By the time Williams moved into City Hall on C Street, he found only a few council colleagues who shared his zeal for urban renewal. Tom Hom, his predecessor, became a vocal leader in the move to renovate the historic Gaslamp Quarter, and Allen Hitch, another councilman, had proposed a San Francisco-style plan for developing the downtown waterfront. His own mentor, Mayor

Curran, was a downtown supporter, but he lost his re-election bid in 1971 and had to push for improvements from the sidelines, as director of the Central City Association.

Centre City was going to need a lot more focus, determination, and, above all, financial investment to restore its vitality. Williams, whose district included downtown at the time, was distressed that many city officials – both staff and political figures – didn't appear to notice or care. Like Nero fiddling while Rome burned, they seemed to shrug their shoulders and accept the fact that downtown was going down in flames.

Williams recalled that the opinions of fellow councilman Jim Ellis typified that laissez faire attitude. "He didn't see why merchants couldn't move to Mission Valley or Mission Bay. He thought that if merchants couldn't keep things going on, we should just let things fall apart."[4]

Even protecting Centre City's existing amenities was a challenge. In the weeks after arriving at City Hall, he was surprised to learn that city bureaucrats had contemplated the sale of Pantoja Park. This green space – named for Spanish explorer Don Juan Pantoja y Arriola, who first mapped San Diego Bay – had been created in 1850, making it the oldest park in San Diego. Williams fought against any suggestion that Pantoja Park was just another piece of real estate. The sale idea was dropped. Once downtown renewal was under way, Pantoja Park became a vital part of the renewing urban fabric. The historic landmark was expanded to include the roadways on three sides, with public access continuing on G Street. It became the green centerpiece for some of the first condos built in the initial wave of downtown redevelopment.

Meanwhile, Williams did what he could to stop – or at least show his disapproval for –the downtown exodus. It was particularly troubling to lose the city's major newspapers. Copley Newspapers had come to City Hall with plans to move the offices of the morning daily, the *San Diego Union*, and its afternoon sister newspaper, the *Evening Tribune*, from their Second Avenue downtown location to a new facility on the north side of Interstate 8. Several years earlier, James C. Copley, the owner and publisher, contributed $200,000 to help fund construction of the new City Hall a few steps from the downtown newspaper offices. Williams wondered what had happened in the intervening period to cause Copley to move his reporters away from the hub of local politics. Whatever the reasons, Williams did not think it was a good idea. "I was the only one to vote against their application for a conditional use permit to move to Mission Valley," Williams said.

His lone dissent failed to stop the newspapers from relocating in October 1973. But it helped define Williams's bigger goal. "Nobody told me that they shouldn't go. I just thought that downtown should be alive."[5]

Even while businesses moved to the suburbs, some city planners and pro-renewal interests agreed with Williams's point of view and continued to hold out hope for downtown. San Diegans Inc., a nonprofit group created in 1959, hired Western Real Estate Research Corp. to conduct a $35,000 economic study of downtown and, with results in hand, lobbied city officials to plan for residential construction and commercial development.[6]

In the late 1950s, city planners also began focusing on downtown renewal. Max Schmidt recalled his special assignment shortly after joining the city's Planning Department in 1956. Then Planning Director Harry Haelsig chose Schmidt and three other city planners to work exclusively on a downtown redevelopment plan, neighborhood by neighborhood. At the time, city offices still operated in the County Administration Center, and the team was cloistered at the top of the building's central tower. The planners, who dubbed their temporary workplace the "ivory tower," began sketching out different project areas, starting with Columbia and Harborview in the Little Italy neighborhood.[7] However, many of their concepts would be stuck in neutral for years, awaiting the political forces that finally moved them forward.

OFF THE DRAWING BOARD AND ONTO THE STREETS

Reviving downtown – to make it desirable for living and doing business again – would require more than a grand planning vision. It would take a new process that could bring those plans to life. It would take millions in private investments. But who was going to spend big bucks constructing a building that was likely to lose value as its neighborhood declined all around it? Williams believed that only serious, concerted intervention – business and government working together – could point Centre City toward its rightful destiny.

Williams began meeting with downtown real estate and business owners, exchanging information and ideas. Among Williams's earliest supporters was George A. Scott, owner of Walker-Scott Department Stores. They hit it off so well that Scott worked on Williams's campaign in his first election in 1969. At the time, Scott's anchor store on Broadway was losing customers to the suburbs, although Scott opened a new department store at the College Grove Center in an effort to keep up with the rapidly changing demographics. He was a respected civic leader, the Rotary Club's Mr. San Diego in 1972, and Mr. San Diego wanted Williams to help reverse the decline of the Centre City.

Williams recalled how Scott came to his City Council office to discuss strategies for convincing developers and other businesses to invest again in downtown. At the time, there weren't many incentives. The two men thought one possible option was using a California community redevelopment law that had been on the state's books for decades. In 1945, the Legislature passed a law allowing local governments to create redevelopment agencies, and six years later, the law was strengthened, enabling a city to generate the funding and land acquisition powers necessary to put teeth into redevelopment. The extra property taxes generated within the borders of a redevelopment area could be recycled to finance improvements and fund more projects.[8]

Based on the state law, San Diego had created a redevelopment agency in 1958, with the City Council acting as its board of directors. But in its early years, the agency's activities were limited despite the best efforts of the city's Planning Department. The problem was the awkward disconnect between city planners and the City Manager's Office, which was responsible for implementing their plans.[9] The grandest blueprint for downtown meant nothing unless the city manager had the motivation and permission from the City Council to complete the projects.

Out of Williams's conversations with Scott emerged the outlines of a way to remove redevelopment activities from the bureaucracy and establish a nonprofit urban renewal arm for the city. Under this arrangement, planners and implementers could work in sync outside City Hall. The new agency would be nimble enough to form public-private partnerships and bring the city's renewal projects to fruition. "We just came up with the idea of creating this redevelopment agency," recalled Williams. I didn't know of anybody who had done it at the time, but I took it to the council."[10]

The dynamics of this renewal opportunity began emerging in late 1971 as city planners worked out the details of a major 15-block renovation of Horton Plaza and the city's voters prepared to elect a new mayor. In the mayoral primary, incumbent Frank Curran finished third, eliminating him from the general election runoff. The top two finishers were San Diego City Attorney Ed Butler and California Assemblyman Pete Wilson. Williams decided to endorse Wilson, although he was low-keyed about his political support so as not to offend any friends who were backing the Democrat, Ed Butler. "I liked Ed, but I just thought Pete Wilson would be better at getting things done," recalled Williams. "Pete had a lot of ties to Republican business leaders, and we were going to need them if we were going to redevelop downtown."[11]

After Pete Wilson was elected mayor in November 1971, he almost immediately showed his support for the first redevelopment plan to come before him on the City Council—the Plaza project. The proposal entailed a $170 million revitalization of a 15-block area around Horton Plaza Park and encompassed the scruffy area bounded by Broadway, G Street, Fourth Avenue and Union Street. The concept had strong backing from the entire City Council and the business community. The depth of that support grew out of disgust with the condition of Horton Plaza, the small park that had stood at the heart of downtown San Diego since one of the city's original developers, Alonzo Horton, created it in 1870. Horton Plaza, once admired for its raffish charm, had turned into a public embarrassment. Its increasingly dangerous underground restroom attracted an assortment of drug addicts, homeless loiterers, and gang members.

But how was the city going to drum up the millions needed to rebuild the infrastructure? Who was going to invest it? Williams was more certain than ever that it was going to take a new agency outside the city's bureaucracy to make it happen. And he was not sure of the new mayor's commitment to the kind of investment it was going to take. The frugal mayor sometimes seemed to show disdain for the streets around City Hall. "Pete Wilson was saying that downtown was a tax eater," Williams recalled.[12]

That was true, of course. The Centre City was in a tailspin. Employers were folding up their tents, moving to the suburbs, and taking their employees and tax base with them. Yet Williams wanted to generate some hard facts showing that the new suburbs north of Interstate 8 were the real tax guzzlers. Because these communities were being built in previously undeveloped areas, they had a voracious appetite for tax-funded infrastructure—roads, schools, police and fire services, parks and libraries.

Williams asked Kimball Moore, the city manager, to prepare a report on the city's Capital Improvement Program. The results showed what Williams suspected. The new developments were gobbling up the bulk of the city's infrastructure resources, while Centre City and older neighborhoods received a few measly crumbs.

The mayor, a moderate Republican, had come into office on a platform of managing the leapfrog residential developments popping up in the outskirts. The report Williams had requested expanded the picture to show the areas left behind – the Centre City and older neighborhoods losing their stores and other businesses to the outer fringes of the city. Not only was growth sprawling out of control, it was sucking up capital improvement money and leaving the other half of the city to languish. Limiting growth and requiring developers to pay for their roads and fire stations was only one side of the equation. Controlled growth policies needed to be balanced with municipal assistance to the forgotten parts of the city. Williams could point to the figures in that capital improvement report and assert that redevelopment would not only improve the aesthetics of the Centre City, it could revive its tax base, making the city financially healthier.

"After that, Pete Wilson began saying that downtown is a tax eater—but we have to make it a tax producer. Pete began selling it to other people, including the Republican power brokers," recalled Williams.[13] The mayor had caught sight of the big picture. And with Wilson at the helm of city government, Williams could see that downtown redevelopment finally had the leadership it needed.

In 1975, the City Council approved creation the Centre City Development Corp. (CCDC), a nonprofit corporation serving as the city's renewal arm. Twenty years later, with the advantage of hindsight, the CCDC board presented Williams with a special directors' award for efforts that "resulted in the beginning of downtown's redevelopment program."[14]

Unshackled from the city bureaucracy, CCDC inched forward its first year until the City Council, acting as the Redevelopment Agency, hired Gerald Trimble as its executive vice president in 1976. Williams strongly supported this choice. "He seemed very competent and determined," recalled Williams. "He was ready to go." Trimble more than met those expectations, and the die was cast for a new age of downtown redevelopment.

Like Williams, Trimble blamed the decline of downtown on suburban sprawl. "What killed San Diego is what killed city after city after city across the country – the easy route," Trimble once told Partners for Livable Places, which supported downtown renewal.

"People moved to the suburbs. Department stores moved to the suburbs. It was easy, cheap land. It was the easy way to do it."[15]

Trimble, on the other hand, relished the challenges of downtown renewal. Tenacious as a pit bull, he thrived on tough negotiations and the thrill of closing a deal.

Meanwhile, thanks to city planners' earlier efforts, CCDC quickly divided the Centre City into manageable geographical areas– the Columbia and Marina districts, Harborview (Little Italy), Cortez Hill, the Gaslamp District, and Centre City East. The Horton Plaza project area remained separate in the CCDC structure.

The massive projects – Horton Plaza and the convention center– had plenty of obstacles and setbacks. Yet, once city leaders embarked on their downtown plan, they found a way to make them happen. Notably, in 1981, downtown renewal opponents forced a referendum on the city's plans for a $224 million convention center proposed for a six-block area in the Columbia District downtown. The anti-convention center contingent rejoiced when San Diego voters rejected the project in a mail-in ballot. But their euphoria was short-lived. Almost immediately, Mayor Wilson and other convention center supporters began pursuing a different strategy. Two years later, the proposed convention center site had been relocated to port property on the bay. The port would finance the construction by selling certificates of participation, which would be repaid with port revenues. This funding mechanism did not require voter approval, but city leaders decided to put the measure on the ballot anyway. This time, voters approved the $164 million convention center project.

Once constructed, the convention center's site on the bay proved a blessing for the 16.5-block Gaslamp Quarter District, which was easy walking distance from the new facility. Thousands of convention-goers and tourists poured into the Gaslamp Quarter's restaurants, clubs and shops. The convention center obstacle not only had been overcome, its relocation improved the dynamics of Centre City's blossoming economy.

BURNISHING SAN DIEGO'S HISTORIC GEMS

History buffs and preservationists wanted to make sure that this newfound juggernaut of redevelopment would not crush important historic gems. Their fears were understandable. For example, the county courthouse built in 1961 replaced a majestic Italianate-style structure that had occupied its downtown site since 1889. When it was built, a 10-foot golden statue of Justice had stood atop its stately bell and clock tower, and statues of four U.S. presidents had adorned it. But due to earthquake concerns, the building at Broadway and Front was altered over the years and demolished in

1959 to make way for a boxy, purely functional courthouse. Forty-two stained glass windows from the old structure, each one representing a different state of those existing in 1890, are on display in local courthouses, a reminder of an era that valued grand architecture and public art.

The San Diego County Courthouse (circa 1915)
Image used courtesy of the San Diego History Center

Williams wanted to take steps to protect the city's historic heritage. "When I was chairman of the Public Facilities and Recreation Committee, the city manager actually suggested that we should tear down the Ford Building in Balboa Park," he said.[16]

Williams thought that was a terrible idea, and he organized a tour of the Ford Building for his fellow committee members. The structure, built for the 1935 exposition, was drab and shabby. The roof leaked. It needed extensive and costly work. Yet they could see the inner beauty of its wheel-like architecture and the need to preserve it. Eventually, the city received federal funding to restore the structure. Today it houses the park's Aerospace Museum.

The Ford Building (1935)
Image used courtesy of the San Diego History Center

Balboa Park had many other treasures worth maintaining. Among them were the eye-catching, ornate buildings in Spanish and Mediterranean styles had been built during the 1915-1916 California-Panama Exposition. They were part of the city's identity. The councilman was deeply concerned that some people seemed to think they were simply old structures that needed to go. He became an ally of a citizens' group, the Committee of 100, which had been formed in 1967. Under its first president Bea Evenson and its second, Patricia DeMarce, the Committee of 100 raised funds to preserve and restore the crumbling Spanish Colonial buildings in the park. In 1968, voters approved a bond measure supported by the group to rebuild the deteriorated Food and Beverage Building. It was approved, enabling the building's reconstruction as the Casa del Prado.

One by one, the other historic buildings and the Spreckels Organ Pavilion were built and restored. And as long as Williams was on the council, the committee could count on his support. "Bea Evenson loved me," said Williams. "She was always inviting me to luncheons and her other events."[17]

The Food and Beverage Building
Image used courtesy of the San Diego History Center

Meanwhile, the move for preservation advanced in the Centre City. One major step to help save downtown history came in 1976 when the City Council adopted the Gaslamp Quarter Urban Design and Development Manual, setting the guidelines for renewing 16.5 blocks lined with Victorian and Art Deco structures. In the following years, its buildings were renovated and recycled as shops, offices, restaurants, and museums.

The historic Balboa Theatre
Image used courtesy of the San Diego History Center

There were other notable historic structures that needed extra protection to survive. Williams worked with Max Schmidt, who was a city planner for 20 years before moving over to head planning efforts at CCDC. The councilman advocated for protections Schmidt had written into the CCDC bylaws for a handful of significant historic structures—the Balboa and Spreckels theaters, the Golden West Hotel on Fourth Avenue, and the Spanish-style Santa Fe Depot down near the waterfront.[18] It was particularly difficult to save and recycle the domed Balboa Theatre. Built in 1926, the Balboa was already an architectural survivor by the time CCDC began working with it. The Balboa had been slated for demolition in 1959 but was rescued and converted into a movie theater. In 1972, the Balboa Theatre was named a local historic site. CCDC bought the theater, although it took years to renovate it and make it earthquake-proof enough for its next incarnation.

REDEVELOPING SOUTHEASTERN SAN DIEGO

By the early 1980s, Williams could see that CCDC was going full throttle. It was acquiring properties, clearing away blight, upgrading aged utilities, and offering incentives that attracted investors and developers. Builders who made their fortunes in the suburbs were persuaded to become major players in the emerging downtown. Ernest Hahn, famous for his shopping centers, developed Horton Plaza shopping center downtown. He eventually delivered an urban open-air marketplace with breath-taking, tiered architecture designed by Jon Jerde. It looked nothing like his sprawling suburban malls, and its uniqueness attracted San Diegans and tourists immediately after opening in 1985. Meanwhile, the quintessential suburban housing developer Pardee built some of the first condominiums –the Park Row complex – next to Pantoja Park.

Williams wanted to use the same powers to help revive Southeastern San Diego. And he encountered no resistance from his colleagues when he proposed a redevelopment agency for its neighborhoods. With City Council approval, the Southeast Economic Development Corporation (SEDC) was created in 1981. The 7.2-square-mile nonprofit, public benefit entity included 15 neighborhoods and was bounded by state Highway 94, Interstate 5, and 69th Street. There were four redevelopment project areas – Central Imperial, Gateway Center West, Mount Hope, and Southcrest plus the Dells Imperial Study Area. Williams turned to a savvy downtown investor and developer, Walter Smyk, to head SEDC's first board.

The potential for developing tax-generating projects in SEDC's redevelopment was more limited than in the dense-packed Centre City. Nevertheless, Williams saw plenty of opportunity for SEDC to partner with private investors and generate more value in these communities. He saw how the railroad right-of-way the city had bought for a trolley could be developed into housing and commercial centers. The developments could be clustered around the stops planned for the line traversing Southeastern San Diego.

He thought of the empty land left in Southcrest after Caltrans abandoned its plans to build Highway 252. Others passed the vacant former highway corridor and saw an ugly field of weeds, dotted with discarded bottles and litter. But when Williams looked over the land, he saw a bright field of dreams – new homes, stores, parks, and restaurants. Over the years, SEDC – through its incentives and partnerships — made that happen.

In 1982, Williams was elected to the Board of Supervisors, where he no longer participated as a member of the city Redevelopment Agency overseeing the construction activity unleashed through CCDC and SEDC. But he could watch the progress from across town at the County Administration Center. Even from that more remote vantage, he could contribute to the newfound synergy. On his recommendation, the county placed its social service offices in the trolley headquarters building. It gave the public a location easily accessed by bus and trolley, and it gave San Diego Trolley an important tenant to occupy its available office space.

A BLOW AGAINST REDEVELOPMENT

Over the years, Williams watched as redevelopment transformed the Centre City and generated jobs, affordable housing, and amenities previously missing from Southeastern San Diego. There were occasional setbacks, and both renewal agencies encountered personnel controversies – an alleged conflict of interest at CCDC and some salary self-dealing at SEDC. But Williams viewed those as fixable issues, a matter of bringing in new management.

How could anyone look at downtown San Diego and conclude there was something wrong with the redevelopment effort? The results were there, spelled out in rebar and concrete, dollars and cents, and in a population topping 40,000 and still growing.

In February 2014, the *U-T San Diego* newspaper looked at the downtown revenue picture and concluded that the Centre City had indeed become a tax producer, not a tax eater. The newspaper stated, "Focusing just on certain areas of the [city's] $2.6 billion budget where community needs can vary widely, it appears that downtown-generated revenues of more than $132 million exceed expenses by roughly $57 million."[19]

Unfortunately, the success of redevelopment attracted the wrong kind of attention during a time of severe recession. Hit with big state budget deficits, California Governor Jerry Brown looked for sources of revenue to plug a huge funding gap for schools and other services. His gaze fell on the redevelopment agencies that had popped up around the state. From Sacramento, these redevelopment-minded cities looked like a patchwork quilt of local jurisdictions hoarding tax revenues for their building projects. Renewal agencies could keep the extra tax revenue generated by improving the value of projects in their area. The taxes going for other services remained frozen at pre-improvement levels. To redevelopment critics, that seemed to rob schools and other services of the growing tax revenues generated by renewal. At the urging of Gov. Brown, the state legislature revoked the California Redevelopment Act, and in February 2012, local renewal agencies lost the tax increment tools and other powers that the state had granted them decades earlier.

For Williams, the loss was a terrible setback. The state's redevelopment law had enabled San Diego officials to rescue and transform the Centre City. It had brought jobs, housing, and new businesses to older neighborhoods. True, the city had created Civic San Diego, a nonprofit agency, to continue the renewal projects that had been under way. But tax increment funding – the rocket fuel of redevelopment – was a thing of the past.

Williams could not believe that Jerry Brown, a fellow Democrat who had been helpful to San Diego over the years, would strike this blow against an effective redevelopment tool. He felt betrayed. "My friend – Jerry," he sighed.

*Invitation to the dedication of the
SDSU Transit Center (2011)*

CHAPTER 7

On Track with Public Transit

On a bright winter day of blue skies and temperatures in the 70s, Leon Williams meets me at the transit headquarters downtown for a tour of the San Diego trolley system he helped create. He will show me how far these tracks have come – and how far they still must go. We are joined by Tom Larwin, retired general manager of San Diego's transit system and a key official in planning and building the San Diego Trolley.

For nearly three decades, Williams was a mover and shaker on the Metropolitan Transit Development Board (later changed to Metropolitan Transit System), making decisions along with his fellow board members that fostered the development of a fixed rail network admired around the nation. His skill as a quiet consensus builder helped keep the project from derailing – always a possibility when dealing with several different jurisdictions and a number of interests with conflicting goals or outright opposition.

During Williams's years with the transit agency, the trolley experienced phenomenal growth. It went from zero to three trolley lines (four counting the Silver Line that loops around downtown), with 53 stations. It blazed a trail for modern North American light-rail systems and was emulated by other cities all over the United States. Ridership on the trolleys and Metropolitan Transit buses rose to a record 95 million passenger trips by the end of fiscal 2014.[1]

On this day, Williams is showing his pride by wearing a baseball hat commemorating an award from the American Public Transportation Association. The organization had named San Diego's Metropolitan Transit the most outstanding large public transit system in the nation.

We board an electric-powered Orange Line trolley. Our light-rail vehicle is a recent model, a Siemens-built S70, immaculately clean and air-conditioned, with a wheelchair-friendly low floor. As we pull out of the station, there is hardly a sound, although its shiny red exterior makes a bold statement against the dull tan, gray, and green of the passing landscape.

The trolley glides easily along the tracks, heading toward Southeastern San Diego, past old commercial buildings and warehouses and then past residential neighborhoods drowsing in the sun. It stops at 25th, 32nd, 47[tth] streets, Euclid and Encanto, offering a brief glimpse of the separate personalities of each area. Then the trolley moves on to the distinct worlds of Lemon Grove, La Mesa, and El Cajon, where we switch to the Green Line.

We push east again to the terminus, the Santee Trolley Square shopping center, and begin our return trip through Mission Valley. A marvel of engineering, the Green Line trolley crisscrosses the San Diego River. It is elevated on bridges above the valley floor and above the 100-year floodplain — presumably keeping the tracks high and dry in times of extreme deluge.

Some of the stations are a study in contrasts. After leaving the stop at Alvarado Hospital, the line swings through a 4,000-foot tunnel that delivers passengers to the underground San Diego State University station.

The next stop – the Grantville Station – is a visible landmark, soaring 40 feet above the homes and businesses of Mission Gorge. Its design inspired one commenter on Yelp, a public review website, to say it looks like "some kinda blue crystal space station" dominating the landscape of Mission Gorge.[2]

The trolley continues its route through the valley, past the historic San Diego Mission, Qualcomm Stadium, and the valley's busy shopping centers – Mission Valley Center, Hazard Center, and Fashion Valley. At the Old Town station, the trolley turns south, circling back through downtown along the bayside route, ending where we started at the 12th & Imperial Transit Center.

Despite its beauty and tranquility, this trip reminds these passengers of the rollercoaster journey required to build the light rail and keep it running smoothly.

We pass by the Qualcomm Stadium trolley station, where thousands of San Diego Chargers fans arrive for home football games. Larwin remembers how in 1998, when San Diego hosted the Super Bowl at Qualcomm Stadium, the trolley system suffered a power failure hours before the start of the nationally televised game. With a lot of scrambling, the power was restored in time for trolley-riding football fans to get to the stadium before kickoff, and a public relations disaster was averted.

Meanwhile, Williams is flooded with memories of the battles that preceded construction of the beautiful Mission Valley trolley line. Doubters and outright opponents had to be persuaded. They did not believe that the trolley would become an exceptional civic asset. Some had tried to block certain routes because they worried it might devalue their residential property or affect their businesses.

Some complained it was bound to become an expensive boondoggle. "There were powerful people who asked me, 'Why are you doing this? It's a waste of time,'" says Williams.

Even some retailers were skeptical. At the popular Fashion Valley station, he is reminded that in the pre-trolley days, some shopping center administrators doubted that they would see benefits from the trolley stopping at the edge of the mall parking lot. One had summed up his skepticism by saying, "Trolley riders are not shoppers."

During the planning and approval phase, some of the greatest obstacles had been the most intangible and difficult to counter – irrational fears of crime, for instance. To Williams, it seemed that opponents had suffered a failure of imagination, their anxiety blinding them to the reality of light-rail transit. Instead of a valuable amenity, the trolley seemed to them like a red dagger pointed at the heart of their communities. It made no sense to Williams, but he had to deal with it, often by amassing an arsenal of facts to bolster his case.

A group of residents from the eastern end of Mission Valley had attended transit agency board meetings, complaining that burglars would take the light rail to their homes so they could steal their TVs. Williams looks around the light-rail car, trying to visualize the absurdity of a burglar loaded down with televisions, hauling his loot home on the trolley. He suspects some of the early critics may have harbored racial and socioeconomic biases and simply didn't want "those people" (the poor, especially minorities) to invade their communities aboard a new mass transit system. "I remember a man at one of our meetings complaining, 'There ought to be someplace where people with money can live,'" Williams says, his expression visibly annoyed.

Another frequent preconstruction complaint was that the trolley would be too noisy. On board the trolley, we discuss the subject easily over the low hum of the moving car, proving that Williams was right to allay those concerns. The trolley car is quiet enough for a conversation. Outside, when we transfer from one trolley line to another, the sounds of the trolleys pulling into a station are muted, fading into the urban landscape.

During the San Diego Trolley's development, San Diego mayors and Metropolitan Transit board members came and went. But year after year, decade after decade, Williams sat on the transit agency board, using his persuasive powers to rally support and help keep the project on track. Williams — the even-tempered strategic thinker — had confidence that the trolley was moving in the right direction, and removing any political or administrative roadblocks would absorb his attention until he retired. Now, as the trolley whisks us around San Diego, he could see that it was worth his years of devotion.

BIRTH OF THE MODERN TROLLEY

During Williams's early career on the San Diego City Council, the notion of creating a regional transit system was just starting to take shape. In 1966 – three years before Williams took office – San Diego voters approved a measure allowing the city of San Diego to acquire the privately owned San Diego Transit bus company and run it as a nonprofit. The city made the purchase the following year, at a time when the bus company was in a financial crisis and struggling to keep pace with the city's rapid suburban growth. Local governments began to realize they would have to step in to preserve reliable public transportation in the future.

Williams thought that improving public transit should be a top priority in a city with 372 square miles and a population increasingly scattered to its farthest edges. He favored some type of fixed guideway system. So did his friend, Jim Mills, a California state legislator for two decades, including 10 years as president pro tem of the California State Senate. In his youth, Mills had ridden the electric-powered trolleys that had been a public transit fixture on the streets of San Diego early in its history. The quaint, charming trolley cars had been replaced with buses, thought to be more modern and flexible, and the last of San Diego's trolleys was retired in 1949. Now, the thinking was coming full circle, and a technologically advanced fixed rail system seemed attractive for fast-growing San Diego.

Williams knew that Mills was in a good position to push for and deliver state funding, and he could sponsor legislation helpful to San Diego's mass transit future. During the 1970s, he would travel to Sacramento to talk transit with Mills. The two men – both Democrats — would lunch at a vegetarian restaurant. Neither ate meat. Instead, they whetted their appetites on a vision of ushering San Diego into a golden age of fixed rail mass transit.[3] Each would play an essential role in making the dream a reality.

The move toward a San Diego regional transportation system was slow out of the starting gate. Mills sponsored the bill that created the Metropolitan Transit Development Board, the agency that would develop San Diego's light-rail system. His original legislation included all of San Diego County. But North County officials opted out, wanting to keep control over their own public transit activities.

MTDB finally started operations in 1976 – without North County but at least with representation from major players, including the city of San Diego, San Diego County, and other communities in the East County and South Bay. Williams was appointed as one of the original four MTDB members from the city of San Diego. Also on the eight-member board were his San Diego council colleagues, Jess Haro, Maureen O'Connor, and Mayor Pete Wilson.

"In the beginning, we weren't quite sure what we would do," said Williams, remembering those days of confusion over which fixed rail options to pursue.

MTDB would soon find its footing, oddly enough, because of a natural disaster. In September 1976, Hurricane Kathleen hit the San Diego & Arizona Eastern Railway with fierce winds and floods, destroying sections of the tracks along with the desire of owner Southern Pacific to keep operating it. Seeking to cut its losses, Southern Pacific moved to abandon the trouble-plagued short-haul line, which extended east from San Diego, dipped into Mexico and ended at Plaster City in Imperial County.

The railroad company's misfortune turned into an opportunity for MTDB. The transportation agency, with San Diego Councilwoman Maureen O'Connor taking the lead, purchased the short-haul railway in 1979. The deal, negotiated by MTDB's attorney Paul Peterson of the law firm Peterson & Price, included more than 100 miles of tracks and right-of-way property, for $18.1 million. That amount included the cost of fixing the storm-damaged tracks.

Williams enthusiastically supported the rail line purchase, which opened up the possibility of building a light-rail public transit system along its tracks. In addition, MTDB could earn extra revenue by leasing SD&AE tracks to a private short-haul railway.

Progress on the trolley came quickly. The first light-rail line between San Diego and San Ysidro on the border with Mexico cost a relatively inexpensive $86 million, all of it from state and local funding. The total included the purchase of the SD&AE line. The 15.4-mile line started operating in 1981, only two years after the SD&AE Railway purchase. The project was hastened by a deadline for using state transit money and by the ease of construction on tracks the agency already owned.

Almost as soon as the light rail service started running, it earned the nickname the Tijuana Trolley in the local media. Williams and his fellow board members were uncomfortable with this instant branding. True, the trolley went to the border, but Tijuana wasn't even in the United States. The MTDB board voted to call it the San Diego Trolley. "[Councilwoman] Maureen O'Connor came up with the idea of painting it red," said Williams. "Maureen said, 'Let's paint this thing red, Leon. We got to paint this thing red. And it has been the San Diego Trolley — and it has been red — ever since."[4]

Five years after service began on the trolley line to the border, the first section of the Orange Line between San Diego and Euclid Avenue began service, and the extension to El Cajon was completed in 1989. The trolley project was on a roll. San Diego's top political figures were lobbying enthusiastically for more funding, including Pete Wilson, who at the time was in the U.S. Senate, Roger Hedgecock, who succeeded Wilson as mayor, and San Diego City Councilman (later San Diego's mayor) Dick Murphy, who chaired the MTDB and traveled to Washington with MTDB general manager Tom Larwin to lobby Congress for trolley financing. These efforts helped bring in the first federal funding. It was used for the El Cajon extension.

In 1985, Murphy left the City Council and the MTDB to become a Superior Court judge. Williams thought that Jim Mills, who had left the state Senate and returned to San Diego, would be the ideal choice to succeed Murphy as MTDB chairman. Williams appreciated Mills's contributions to San Diego's expanding light rail system, including the state funding Mills had funneled into public transportation. That year, Mills took the position and held it for the following nine years.

During Mills's tenure, one of the frustrations was MTDB's inability to move forward with construction of a proposed line that was supposed to include service to the University of California, San

Diego (UCSD). The planned 11-mile Mid-Coast Corridor line was to start at the Old Town station, stop at UCSD, and continue to University Town Centre in La Jolla.   But MTDB hit a roadblock.

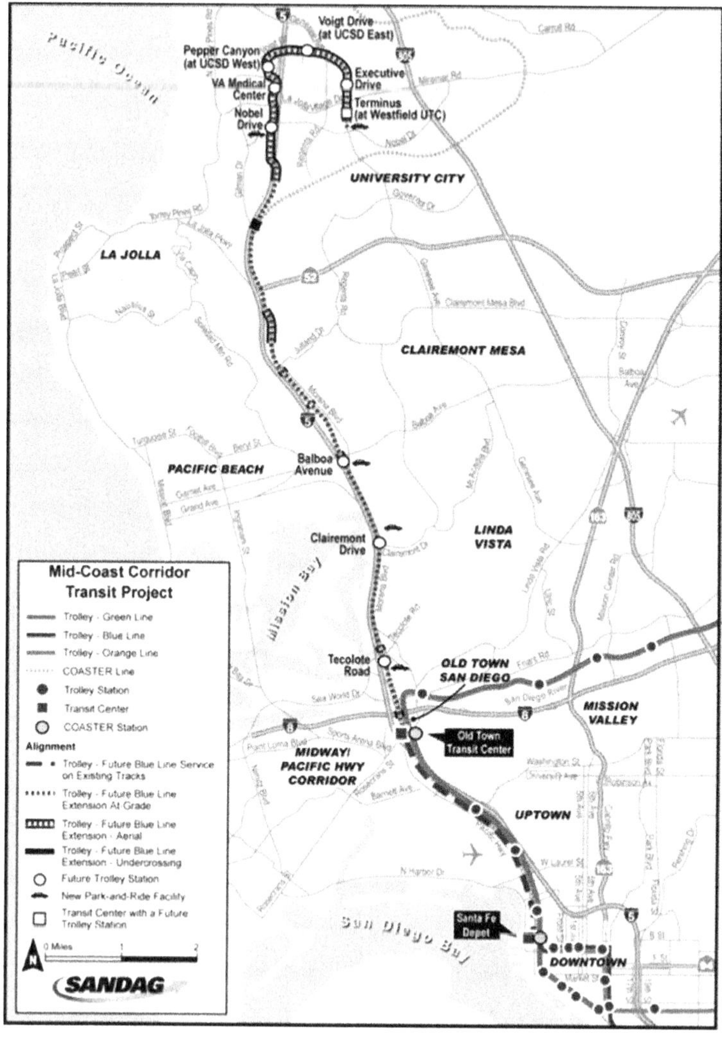

Map of the planned Mid-Coast Corridor

Richard Atkinson, UCSD's chancellor from 1980 to 1995, opposed extending the trolley onto the UCSD campus. Tom Larwin, then the MTDB general manager, recalled an MTDB meeting, which Atkinson and a retinue of UCSD representatives attended in order to raise objections to proposed trolley routes. Larwin recalled that Atkinson told MTDB officials that he did not want the trolley line to cross through the campus because, among other things, it might bring in rapists. They came with a host of other issues as well, such as the concern that the trolley line would conflict with plans for constructing future buildings on campus.

Williams, who was MTDB's vice chairman at the time, said he and chairman Jim Mills visited Atkinson twice in an effort to win his support for the trolley extension and assure him the station would benefit the campus and its students. But none of these arguments persuaded the chancellor, who had an objection for every argument in favor. "He said the trolleys' vibrations would disturb the university's instruments," recalled Williams. "We even offered to put the trolley underground. It seemed like he was looking for excuses to say no." After Atkinson refused to budge, Williams was surprised that Mills began to oppose the Mid-Coast Corridor trolley line.[5]

But there was plenty of pro-trolley pressure from other quarters. San Diego congressmen Bill Lowery and Jim Bates were pushing the university to get behind the trolley extension so that they could request federal funding for preliminary studies.[6]

Gradually, UCSD softened its opposition. In 1990, at the first Mid-Coast Corridor Transit Improvement Study meeting, UCSD spokesman Milton Phegley read from a policy statement: "UCSD's support for an extension of the trolley cannot be overemphasized."[7] The route that UCSD officials favored was an alignment down the center of Interstate 5, which Phegley described as offering "greater ridership" and being "the least disruptive to the campus and community."[8] Williams disagreed. The trolley station had to be on campus to make it convenient for students, he believed. Otherwise, not many would ride it.

While debate swirled around the proposed Mid-Coast Corridor line, planning and construction proceeded on a separate route circling from Old Town and heading east through Mission Valley. The first segment stopped at the historic San Diego Mission de Alcala. And plans were in the works for one of the agency's biggest challenges — construction of a $500 million, 5.9-mile trolley extension from the Mission San Diego Alcalá through the east end of Mission Valley.

The proposed extension, the future Green Line, would connect with the Orange Line at the Grossmont Transit Center, and it would continue from El Cajon to Santee.

Mills disagreed with an alignment planned through Santee that would have had the trolley line ending in what was then a dirt lot. Shortly after the board rejected his preference for a Cuyamaca terminus and voted for the location he opposed, Mills resigned from MTDB. The Green Line was going to push far into the East County, and the dirt lot at the trolley's terminus would soon be developed into the Santee Town Center station and the Santee Trolley Square shopping center.

After Mills resigned his chairmanship in 1994, the other board members turned to Williams, the vice-chair, to take over as head of the board. "I had been hoping to take some vacation, do some traveling, maybe motor home around the country," sighed Williams, who was in the process of retiring from his seat on the San Diego Board of Supervisors. He also had looked forward to spending more time with his extended family, including his by-then grown children, Karen, Leon Jr., Susan, and Alisa, his two stepchildren, Jeffrey and Penny, and his wife Margaret's three children by a previous marriage, Lindsay, Gregory and Patricia McQuater. But once again, Williams put his personal dreams on hold to continue his public service. For the most part, his 30-foot motor home stayed parked behind his house. He chaired Metropolitan Transit for nearly a dozen years until December 31, 2005. By that time, he was 83 and had served on the transit board all but one year since its inception in 1976.

For Williams, deferring retirement from the transit board was worth the sacrifice. It meant he could spend a few more years helping MTDB expand the San Diego Trolley light rail system, establish its basic network and develop its ridership, both for locals and visitors. The trolley's red cars already glided along the tracks to the border, circled the Centre City, traveled through Southeastern San Diego, and now the tracks were being installed through another important corridor, Mission Valley.

*Top Transit Officials Celebrate the Mission Valley Light Rail Extension.
Leslie Rogers, Leon Williams, Rodney Slater, Nuria Fernandez, and Tom Larwin*

As the trolley moved ahead, Williams needed facts and statistics that would help him address residents' fears that the trolley would cause an increase in crime. In 1994, at Williams's request, the MTDB had the San Diego Association of Governments prepare an analysis of the crime rates along the trolley line. It was an effort designed to guide the trolley's security needs as well as pierce some of the myths about the trolley bringing criminals into neighborhoods along its route. The study analyzed crime patterns between 1987 and 1991.[9] The trolley stations examined had been built in 1989, so the analysts could crunch the crime rate numbers before and after their construction. The analysis showed some crime issues within 660 feet of the trolley platforms – problems that could be addressed with better security. But beyond the actual stations and their parking lots, there was no evidence that the trolley caused an increase in neighborhood crime. (In June 2009, the San Diego Association of Governments released another study, "Understanding Transit's Impact on Public Safety," that reached a similar conclusion.)[10]

Meanwhile, during his tenure as MTDB chairman, he continued to search for trolley construction funding, lobbying the Clinton Administration for federal money. He met with Rodney Slater, the U.S. Secretary of Transportation at the time. Like Williams, Slater was African American, and Williams found him likable and willing to listen to MTDB's appeal for federal transit funding. "We became friends," said Williams, remembering those visits.

Williams also had solid ammunition to make the case. The trolley MTDB had built was so successful that other cities began building their own light-rail systems.

The San Diego Trolley's Mission Valley east extension was selected as one of a handful of projects nationwide qualifying for major federal funding. In 1999, Congress approved $325 million in funding for the Mission Valley trolley extension.

The most daunting task was figuring out how, along the way, the trolley line could serve San Diego State University. SDSU had more than 30,000 students plus faculty, employees, and visitors. Stores, apartments, and homes bordered much of the campus. Parking was a colossal headache. What was the best way to improve public transit for this university city on Montezuma Mesa?

Williams – remembering his own experience as an SDSU undergraduate – favored a proposal that would bring the trolley to the middle of the campus, where students would have easy access to classrooms and other buildings. He was appalled that the original MTDB plan called for the university's trolley station to be built next to Interstate 8, in a place involving an arduous trek to the main campus. "It would have attracted almost nobody," he said.

The on-campus plan, however, was complicated. It involved construction of a 4,000-foot tunnel through the heart of the campus, with the station itself strategically located to maximize ridership. There were arguments over the cost, although, as it turned out, constructing the station near the freeway would have been expensive and logistically awkward.

Williams also had to deal with objections from parking interests, which earned money from the parking permits sold for the lots and parking structures on the campus peripheries. Williams thought it was unreasonable for concerns over parking revenues to prevail over the transit interests of the students. Commuters often suffered through long searches for an empty parking space around campus or along the traffic-clogged streets around the university. Even if the trolley put a dent in parking permit revenues, it would give students, faculty and staff, and campus visitors a convenient and much-needed transit alternative. It would help relieve the unbearable traffic congestion and the frayed nerves of professors constantly interrupted by tardy commuter students. Moreover, the trolley gave students living on or around the campus easy access to Mission Valley shopping centers and downtown San Diego. The university also could boast that the trolley created a transportation connection between Mexico and the SDSU campus, boosting its credentials as a hub for U.S.-Mexico studies and relations. In the end, the transit agency agreed to compensate the parking providers for any loss of their parking revenue during construction.

With support from then-SDSU President Stephen Weber, construction began in 1999 for the on-campus trolley station. From an engineering standpoint, the tunnel through the campus proved to be less troublesome than some anticipated. Most of it — 2,915 feet of the tunnel's length – was built with a simple "cut-and-cover" method. The remaining 1,070 feet was bored beneath campus using the innovative New Austrian Tunnel method.[11] Yet, the project was in the middle of a busy university, so construction was stop-and-go, halting periodically whenever school administrators deemed the work too disruptive.

The $103 million underground station – bigger and more elaborate than any other in the San Diego light-rail system – finally opened in 2005. The university community quickly realized this was hardly an ordinary trolley stop. It was a transit tour de force. University, transit, and political leaders praised it, and trolley passes sold like hotcakes.

The SDSU transit center became recognized as a model of efficiency. It consolidated bus and trolley service, with buses on the plaza above the trolley tracks.

It also earned high points for its aesthetics. The trolley station is 55 feet below ground. Passengers ascend by stairs, escalators or a glass-fronted elevator from the track level platforms onto the mezzanine of the station, where light streams around pilasters of gold-colored travertine and through window openings adorned with swirls of decorative wrought iron—public art intended to suggest roots.

The SDSU Trolley Station (2015)

Just outside the exit is a plaza, the Aztec Green, sloping up to the main campus and the gleaming white Conrad Prebys Aztec Student Union. Completed nine years after the trolley station opened, the 194,000-square-foot Mission Revival structure reflects some of the architectural features of the older mission-style buildings on campus, and under its dome, which seems to soar to the heavens, there are restaurants, study lounges, meeting rooms, student services, and even a bowling alley. In their design wisdom, Metropolitan Transit and the university had created a grand gateway into the San Diego State University campus, a place of arrivals and departures near the welcoming doors of a new student union – the campus living room, as the students called it.

In a 2011 ceremony, the SDSU trolley station was dedicated to Leon Williams. Former San Diego City Councilman Harry Mathis, who became MTS board chairman after Williams retired, said, "It is only fitting that we recognize Leon with the dedication of SDSU Station. Without Leon, the trolley may never have made it to campus. Leon insisted on an alignment that came to the heart of campus. And it has been a great success from the very first day." [12]

The plaque dedicating the SDSU Trolley Station to Leon Williams

For Williams, the applause and accolades showered on the completed SDSU trolley station dimmed the memories of the many obstacles along the path to its creation – the questions over its location, the engineering challenges, the financing issues, and the hostility of people who didn't support public transit and thought it was a crazy idea.

Leon Williams at the SDSU Trolley Station dedication (2011)
Photo courtesy of the SDSU Newscenter

Yet his time with MTDB was almost over, and there was more to do. Other transit officials would have to oversee the mission of building the Mid-Coast Corridor light rail line, with its trolley stop at UCSD. That project still had opponents, including Jim Mills, the transit agency board's former chairman who continued to criticize the project after his retirement from MTDB. In a 2006 *U-T San Diego* article, Mills was quoted as saying that there were not enough potential riders to justify construction of the Mid-Coast line. He said that "a bus line should be put in. ...If the time comes when the bus service indicates that a railway is justifiable, then that's the time to build a railway. If the patronage isn't there, that's going to be a real hemorrhage of dollars."[13]

Williams did not agree with that opinion and, shortly after he left the transit board, he spoke out publicly in a column he wrote for the *San Diego Union-Tribune*, stating that the Mid-Coast line "must be built. It needs to be rail, where people have confidence in its scheduling and efficiency."[13]

Nevertheless, he understood the reasoning behind Mills's opposition. Spending vast amounts on a trolley line was always a big gamble. If the finished product attracted few riders, the failure could doom any other proposed trolley extensions, no matter how much they were needed. In fact, MTDB had chosen the trolley line between downtown San Diego and the border to be built first because San Diego Transit's similar bus route boasted high ridership. While some bus officials grumbled that the trolley had cannibalized a high-revenue bus route, Williams figured that the first light-rail line needed to show its success by enticing bus passengers to switch to the trolley.

"Looking back now, maybe [Chancellor] Atkinson did us a favor," said Williams, reflecting on the Mid-Coast extension's long delays.[14] San Diego State University had gone first and demonstrated that a trolley station could be an enormous asset on a big college campus. Besides serving San Diego State, the Green Line had a plethora of busy stops to attract riders, including shopping centers, the football stadium, a hospital and the historic mission. Its healthy ridership improved the odds of obtaining adequate funding for future extensions of the trolley.

The San Diego Association of Governments, which took over MTDB's planning and development in 2003, continued work on the Mid-Coast project, including an extension to UCSD. The planned trolley line now includes two stations serving the UCSD campus, one west of Interstate 5 and the other east of it.

Looking back on his days on the transit board, Williams said he only regretted one decision. It was a mistake, he said, to give the San Diego Association of Governments power over Metropolitan Transit's long-range planning, financial programming and project development. State legislation had authorized the change in 2002, but Williams only went along, he said, because it was supposed to centralize planning not only for transit but for several other countywide agencies such as the Air Pollution Control Board. In theory, putting agencies under the purview of the San Diego

Association of Governments made sense. "Then, the other agencies except transit pulled out, and only the transit agencies were left," he said.[15]

The shift of administrative authority also caused the Metropolitan Transit to lose its general manager, Tom Larwin, who moved over to the San Diego Association of Governments to oversee the transfer of activities from the Metropolitan Transit Development Board to the countywide planning agency. Capable, highly organized and trained as a civil engineer, Larwin had joined the transit agency's staff at the outset and had served as its general manager since 1979. He was in charge of the agency through the trolley construction phase and, later, through the challenges of getting it up and running smoothly. Larwin stayed at the San Diego Association of Governments nearly two years before retiring.

That left Metropolitan Transit rudderless while its board searched for someone to fill Larwin's position. Williams recalled that there was pressure from some fellow board members to diminish the transit agency's top manager position. "I missed a meeting and when I came back, I found out they had lowered the salary they were going to offer," he said. "I said, 'No, you can't do that. We need to be able to attract someone really good.'"[16]

Ultimately, the board hired Paul Jablonski, who had served as president and CEO of the Southwest Ohio Transit Authority. He had been recommended for his leadership and experience. He started his San Diego job as Metropolitan Transit's chief executive officer in January 2004. Under his watch the American Public Transportation Association named San Diego's Metropolitan Transit System the best of America's big transportation systems.

SHAPING A TROLLEY LIFESTYLE

During one of its early meetings in the 1970s, MTDB members were discussing a list of principles for developing a fixed rail project, when Williams spoke up. He wanted to add another principle no one else had mentioned – land use.

While his suggestion did not get a lot of attention at the time, Williams was convinced that a light-rail transit line was much more than a means of getting from Point A to Point B. It could help create a more functional city. He envisioned new residential and commercial developments springing up around the trolley stations, pedestrian malls with trendy restaurants and cafes. There would be park-and-ride lots for commuters and easy connections to their employment. He described this pattern of development as "smart growth."

If a transit agency could get people out of their cars, maybe the city would grow in a denser, healthier, more efficient way. "A fixed rail guideway is always going to be there," he explained. "So it's more likely to attract investments. The investor is going to know that it's not going to go anywhere."[18]

There were plenty of successful public transit models. In the great, densely populated cities of the world — New York, Washington D.C., Paris, London, and Tokyo, among others – residents of different occupations and socioeconomic classes rubbed shoulders on trains, subways, and buses. Driving one's own car in those cities was, and still is, expensive, nerve-wracking, and usually a big time-waster. In San Diego, the trend was just the opposite. During the 1950s and 1960s, the city's rapid growth, with its sprawling residential development hop-scotching around the city's outskirts, was taking San Diego from a city that, in its early days, relied on public transit to a metropolis dependent on cars.

By the time Williams took office in 1969, the network of freeways had influenced the shape of San Diego, creating a car culture based on mobility and convenience. In the growing suburbs that clustered around freeway exits north of Interstate 8, residential cul-de-sacs and big parking lots seemed more important than urban connections.

Buses, of course, remained an important part of the expanding regional transit system, but Williams thought that in a car culture, they were frequently the object of a kind of automotive snobbery. It was commonly believed that buses were only for people who couldn't drive—the elderly, students or people who didn't own a car. Moreover, bus routes could change. By comparison, the trolley and its tracks looked more like a permanent amenity, said Williams.

Once light rail began service in San Diego, Williams recognized that the evolving trolley system, with bus routes feeding into it, was helping to transform perceptions about mass transit. People began to hop aboard the trolleys to get around downtown, commute to work, shop in Mission Valley, attend Chargers' games, bowl games, Padres games, or special events at the convention center. At last, public transit attracted riders who might otherwise have traveled in their cars. "One of the ambitions we always had was to try to induce people to ride who do have a choice," Williams said.[20]

With the trolley gaining popularity, its presence began to attract developers, just as Williams had hoped. In 2004, while Williams was still chairing the MTDB, San Diego officials unveiled a $128.5 million proposal for the quintessential "smart growth" project on the east side of downtown San Diego. Smart Corner, as it was called, replaced a jumble of decrepit structures with a 19-story residential tower and a new five-story office building, purchased by the San Diego Housing Commission. The trolley tracks were reconfigured so that they curved from C Street onto Park Boulevard and passed between the two new buildings on a diagonal path. As with other downtown redevelopment, the financing involved a

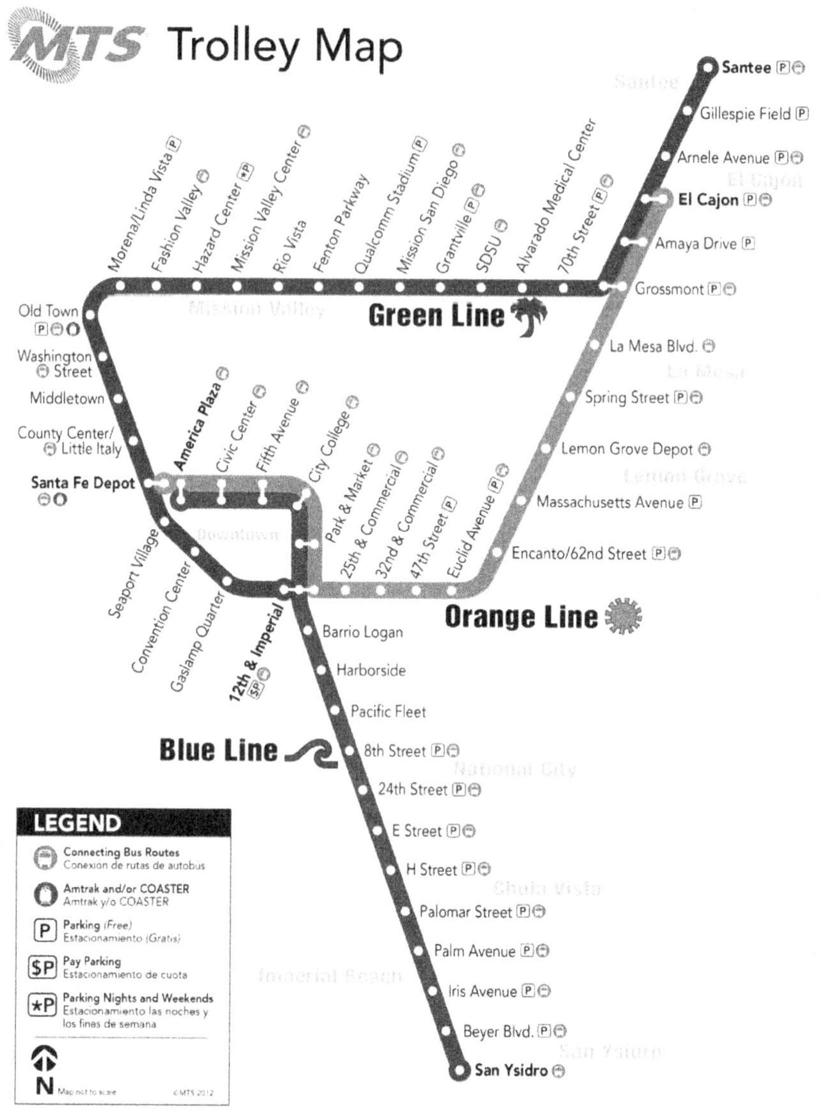

Map of the Trolley Lines (2015)
Image used courtesy of MTS

public and private partnership, including the Centre City
Development Corp., the San Diego Association of Governments,
the San Diego Housing Commission, Metropolitan Transit,
developer Lankford & Associates, and Urban Housing Partners.
The Smart Corner coalition had star power, too. Earvin "Magic"
Johnson was a member of the board of the Canyon-Johnson Urban
Fund, which invested $22.5 million in the project.

All along the trolley lines, other projects, with stores, condos
and apartments, began to appear along the trolley lines. For
instance, the Village at Morena Vista, completed in 2006, created a
new urban center next to the trolley stop at the west end of Mission
Valley, with 185 apartments and 22 loft-style townhomes over stores
and offices covering 18,500 square feet. It was built through a
partnership of Metropolitan Transit, the San Diego Redevelopment
Agency, the city of San Diego and LLC, an affiliate of William
Jones's CityLink Investment Corp.

Another example is Fairfield Residential's housing
developments Alterra and Pravada with 527 apartments and retail
space surrounding La Mesa's Grossmont Trolley Station. In
addition, the city of La Mesa, Metropolitan Transit, and the San
Diego Association of Governments spent nearly $8 million on a
project to build elevators at the station, connecting public transit
with pedestrian walkways, housing and shopping.

In Southeastern San Diego, the nonprofit Jacobs Foundation spearheaded a renewal project near the Orange Line's Euclid trolley station, investing $3.5 million to buy 20 acres and an empty factory. With the foundation underwriting construction costs and the city providing $2 million in tax incentives, the land was redeveloped into a shopping center anchored by a Food 4 Less grocery store.

Even so, Williams had higher expectations, particularly for the other Southeastern San Diego trolley stations. Part of his motivation for backing creation of the Southeast San Diego Development Corporation, a city redevelopment arm, was to have the city use tax incentives and the trolley's right-of-way property as a catalyst for creating new complexes – essentially small, dense villages – in low-income urban areas. But some trolley stops in Southeastern San Diego had not seen major redevelopment. And finding resources to help promote redevelopment would get tougher. For budget reasons, California legislators abolished renewal agencies like the Southeast San Diego Development Corporation throughout the state, cutting off a source of tax increment redevelopment revenue for an area that badly needed it.

Nevertheless, Williams expressed confidence that when community conditions are ripe for new homes, restaurants, and shops, the trolley stations will make it more attractive for future investors. "I see a lot of potential there," he said, smiling.

And he is hopeful that the trolley system will continue to expand and improve over time. He envisions the day when the trolley will serve the communities of Interstate 15 and connect coastal and inland neighborhoods. This wide transportation network, he hopes, could help reshape San Diego into a "city of villages," with all the best of small town life linked to the grand activities at the heart of the city.

Leon Williams with his County Supervisor's Staff
(bottom row)Barbara Terry and Leon Williams
(second row) Jimmy Slack, Isabel Perez, Benelia Santos-Hunter, Margaret
(back row) John Miller, Colleen Carnevale, Hervadine Hoover-Herbin, and
Adrienne Brodeur

Chapter 8

From City to County: The Human Factor

In 1982, Leon Williams decided to leave the City Council and run for a seat on the San Diego County Board of Supervisors. "I thought it was time for a change," said Williams, in his typically understated style. The moment seemed right. The Fourth District county supervisor's seat was coming vacant that year. The incumbent officeholder, Democrat Jim Bates, was running for Congress. Williams, a popular political figure with a ton of name recognition, coasted to victory in the Fourth District Supervisor's election. Once again making history, he became the first African American county supervisor.

Moving to the county meant a shift in the nature of the work. The county government's planning, infrastructure and other public services were primarily limited to the unincorporated areas. But, as an arm of the state, the county government had broad regional jurisdiction over the criminal justice system, social welfare and public health programs, and property tax collection, among other responsibilities. One thing didn't change. Just as in the city of San Diego, Williams wanted to represent the people traditionally excluded, the people forgotten by decision-makers. He wanted to respond to emerging public needs that demanded official attention.

Leon Williams upon winning the County Supervisor election (1982) Image used courtesy of U-T

Williams was ideally prepared to help make policy on the Board of Supervisors. As a former county social worker and administrator at the Sheriff's Department, he had profound knowledge of the county's inner workings. And his years on the council had honed his negotiating skills.

On the Board of Supervisors, he had a higher profile. He was one of five county supervisors, compared with the San Diego City Council, which during his tenure had eight council members and the mayor. On most votes, he only needed to persuade two others to side with him. That was not always easy. Although officially nonpartisan, the Board's majority was Republican, and Williams would have to court conservatives in order to win approval for his proposals.

Williams could not have taken his seat on the Board at a more difficult time. The 1980s presented an array of wrenching social and financial challenges for the county. Federal funding for local community and social welfare programs was drying up. Nevertheless, the county government had to provide indigent health care and legal defense, among other services for the poor.

He had to deal with the emerging deadly threat of AIDS, acquired immune deficiency syndrome, which seemed to come out of nowhere in the early 1980s. It ravaged the gay community, although cases also began to appear among heterosexuals, disproportionately among African Americans and Hispanics. Researchers discovered that the incurable disease could be spread through sexual contact, dirty needles, and blood transfusions. Health officials hastened to get the word out to the public.

At the county level, the Board of Supervisors seemed slow to respond to the crisis. In the mid-1980s, a regional AIDS task force was established to make recommendations to the county. By late 1987, its members were complaining about county inaction. Marguerite Jackson, epidemiology director at UCSD Medical Center, said the "cumbersomeness" of county government prevented it from responding with urgency. Neil Good, Williams's staff assistant, told a *San Diego Union* reporter that Supervisor Leon Williams "shares the frustration a lot of people have regarding the pace and enthusiasm with which the county seems to be responding to the AIDS crisis."[1]

Williams, however, wasn't sitting back and lamenting the lack of progress. He did what he could to bring common sense to an issue fraught with prejudices and misinformation. In June 1987, Williams proposed the creation of a special office within the county's Health Services Department. The Board of Supervisors approved the proposal unanimously.[2] The Office of AIDS Coordination brought together county employees dealing with different aspects of the AIDS crisis, a move designed to maximize the county's response. Williams wanted this new office to focus on education, prevention, and care. He also lobbied for federal AIDS money, traveling to Washington to meet with U.S. Senator Ted Kennedy. And he advocated for a clean needle exchange program to prevent the spread of AIDs among drug addicts.

AIDS was just one of the major issues he tackled during his 12 years on the board. The following are a few examples of how Williams made a difference.

Too small for this world

In the 1980s, cries of desperation rose from the preemie wards, where the county's most vulnerable, neediest babies were being born in ever increasing numbers. Better medical care and technology could keep more of the premature infants alive — but at a huge cost. And if the mothers were indigent, public programs covered the expenses.

Medical experts connected the increase in premature and low birth rate babies under 4.5 pounds to the rising number of mothers who had received little or no prenatal care, a broad term for health care received during pregnancy. No-care moms walked into the hospital in labor, undermining perinatal programs designed to care for women from around the fifth month of pregnancy – the time when a fetus becomes viable — through the days immediately after the delivery of the baby. The problem was growing worse for San Diego County, which had the highest rate of no-care mothers in the state, according to the California Department of Health Services.[3]

The extent of the problem was revealed in a study at the University of California, San Diego Medical Center. Described in a 1986 article in the *American Journal of Obstetrics and Gynecology*, the study concluded that cuts in publicly funded prenatal programs from 1981 to 1984 were responsible for a dramatic increase – from 7.8 percent to 14.9 percent – of babies whose mothers received little or no prenatal care prior to having their babies at the UCSD Medical Center.[4]

The study focused on 100 women who had fewer than three prenatal visits. These no-care moms and their newborns had more unfavorable outcomes and higher medical costs than a control group of 100 mothers who participated in a state-funded perinatal program. The study estimated the extra cost of delivering babies to 400 women with no prenatal care at $877,600. "These results suggest that extension of prenatal care programs to medically indigent women is likely to result in a net reduction in perinatal morbidity and health care expenditures," stated the article on the UCSD Medical Center study.[5]

As the agency paying for indigent health care, county government felt the financial impact of inadequate prenatal services. At the time, county officials reported that the county typically paid UCSD Medical Center about $5 million annually for health care for the uninsured. Of that amount, more than half — $3 million — went for delivering babies.[6]

When Williams was appointed chairman of the Board of Supervisors in 1990, one of his top priorities was to improve access to prenatal and perinatal care. That January, in his state-of-the-county address, he said:

In some cases we spend as much as $60,000 in a matter
of weeks for round-the-clock, intensive medical care for
low-weight babies that were born because their mothers
didn't receive proper care. If we provided them with
proper care in advance, it would only cost $300 to $400.
Not only is this better for the taxpayer, it gives us a
chance to get a productive member of society rather than
somebody who will be dependent on welfare for the rest
of her life. [7]

What could the county do? Williams focused on two
approaches: education and an outreach to the medical community.

As board chairman, Williams led the county's effort to
guarantee Medi-Cal payments within 30 days, with a goal of enticing
more obstetricians to provide perinatal care to the poor. Dozens
refused to see Medi-Cal patients. Not only were the Medi-Cal
reimbursements considered too low by some, but they complained
that the state's Medi-Cal program lagged in getting them the fees
they were owed. Under the new policy, the county paid the
obstetricians quickly and then sought reimbursements from the
slower Medi-Cal state bureaucracy. The county was allowed to tap
into $800,000 of the state's cigarette tax to set up the program.[8]

Williams and Supervisor Brian Bilbray also teamed up to create
a perinatal provider network – representatives from hospitals,

community clinics, doctors, and county officials. The effort was designed to remove barriers that prevented women and their babies from getting perinatal care.

Possibly the toughest challenge was arguing in favor of extending more prenatal and perinatal care to women addicted to drugs or alcohol. These mothers' weaknesses led to an increasing number of "crack babies" and other addicted newborns doomed to painful withdrawal and, in some cases, lives filled with limitations. This was a group of mothers held in public contempt. Yet Williams recognized that reducing the number of sick, drug-addicted infants and, in the process, reducing the amount of public money needed to care for them, was a good idea. That could happen if more of these mothers received prenatal and rehabilitation services rather than punishment, he believed. Williams turned to one of his most effective strategies – rallying experts to make his case. On April 24, 1990, he presided over a two-hour Board of Supervisors' conference during which experienced officials explained the need to help drug-abusing pregnant women. "We're facing a tight budget," said Williams at the time. "but this is a high-priority issue."[9] His board colleagues responded by directing county staff to come up with better ways to deal with the problem.

Williams often appealed to his conservative Board of Supervisors colleagues on the cost benefits of prenatal care. It was an effective political argument. Yet, at a personal level, Williams often thought of how this investment in maternal health could lower the number of suffering infants and parents who faced the agonizing heartbreak of birth defects, low birth weight problems, even infant mortality – and that was something that could not be measured in dollars and cents.

EDUCATING YOUNG DADS

While the prenatal care programs focused on future moms, Williams believed it was also important to engage the fathers. Too often, they were adolescents without an inkling of their paternal duties and expectations. So Williams supported parenting classes that would educate youngsters on the obligations of fatherhood. Among the programs he backed was Developing Adolescent Dads for Success (DADS), which was made available at San Diego schools. His support for the program earned Williams a Courage to Care award from then Gov. Pete Wilson, the former San Diego mayor. Williams's support for the teen fathers program continued after he retired from the Board of Supervisors. In 1995, the Leon Williams Foundation was among the sponsors of a forum featuring teen parents urging other teens to delay starting a family.[10]

WHERE THERE'S SMOKE, THERE'S IRE

From the outset of his political career, health-conscious Leon Williams believed in creating smoke-free zones for non-smokers. He had to move gradually, step by step, because he and his allies were up against powerful forces. Cigarettes were highly addictive, and even when people wanted to quit, they often failed. The tobacco industry worked non-stop to lure more people into smoking. In those days, the hooked smokers lit their cigarettes almost everywhere.

As a beginning San Diego councilman, Williams found some of his council colleagues unapologetically puffing away during their public meetings. Too polite and too new on the council to demand that they put out their cigarettes, he endured his irritated eyes and throat. A staff member got him a small table fan, which he ran conspicuously during the sessions to clear the air. Gradually, his confidence grew, and he emerged as a leader in adopting smoking restrictions. "The smokers would argue that we were interfering with their rights," said Williams. "I would argue that the non-smokers needed to have their rights respected, too."[11]

He was armed with compelling public health information. Study after study confirmed the hazards of smoking – and even the risks of inhaling second-hand smoke. As early as 1964, the U.S. Surgeon General's Advisory Committee on Smoking and Health concluded that smoking caused cancer and bronchitis.[12] During the following years, new federal laws required a warning on the side of cigarette packages and prohibited cigarette ads on broadcast television.

At the local level, Williams pushed for the city of San Diego's first smoking restrictions, which the council approved in 1975. The ordinance prohibited smoking in public buildings, grocery stores, and buses.

Once he was on the Board of Supervisors, Williams worked to expand smoking restrictions for the county's unincorporated areas. The board approved an ordinance in 1983 that required restaurants with 20 seats or more to create non-smoking areas. It also banned smoking in retail and service establishments. The following year, the ordinance added a provision allowing employees to request a non-smoking work area. (The county's ordinance applied only in unincorporated areas, but the city of San Diego adopted the same smoking restrictions.)

Three years later, Williams was on the move again, proposing an even tougher smoking ban for unincorporated areas. Under the previous regulation, restaurants only had to set aside an undefined space for non-smokers. The new proposal was much more specific, requiring restaurants to set aside half their space for non-smokers. It also banned smoking in health care facilities, except for psychiatric offices and wards.

Williams had to eliminate some of the stricter parts of his proposal in order to get the board majority he needed to pass the ordinance. For instance, bars and lounges were exempted from having to designate half their establishments for non-smokers. His fellow supervisors also rejected a provision requiring new restaurants to be built with totally separate smoking and non-smoking sections. "We were trying to minimize opposition," Williams explained at the time.[13]

Nevertheless, the county's new smoking regulations moved the ball down the playing field, as the public grew more accustomed to the ever-tightening rules of the game. His efforts were recognized and praised by non-smoking advocates. "He was an absolute leader," said Debra Kelley, regional director for the California chapter of the American Lung Association. "He championed smoke-free policies before anyone else was thinking about them."[14]

A RESPECTABLE DEFENSE FOR THE POOR

In 1963, the U.S. Supreme Court handed down a ruling in Gideon v. Wainwright requiring state courts to provide free counsel to criminal defendants who couldn't afford to pay for private attorneys.

But when Williams became a county supervisor, he could see that the indigent defense program in San Diego County wasn't working. In an effort to keep down costs, the Board of Supervisors had created the Office of Defender Services in 1978. The office contracted with outside attorneys and eventually hired a few staff attorneys. Complaints of shoddy representation and attorney conflicts of interest were rolling into the county's Office of Defender Services, and the cost of its operations was escalating. As far as Williams could tell, this system - created to protect the constitutional rights of the accused — was unfair and ineffectual. That point was underscored in a lawsuit filed against the county by the Defenders Program of San Diego, Inc. Among other allegations, the suit accused the county of having a contract with one law firm for $150,000 to cover 2,400 misdemeanor cases in the El Cajon court. That meant an average of $62.50 a case, hardly enough to provide much of a defense.

For Williams, the solution was to create a full-scale Public Defender's Office within the county government. But a board majority - supervisors Brian Bilbray, Susan Golding, and George Bailey - voted to give indigent defense to Community Defenders, a nonprofit public defenders corporation. Williams did not like this option and consistently voted against it. "It seemed wrong that the lawyers doing the prosecuting were part of the county government, but the people doing the defense would not be county employees, and they wouldn't qualify for equal pay or any of the county benefits," he recalled.[15]

At the time, however, he also tried to persuade his board colleagues by arguing that it would be easier to monitor and control costs if the defense attorneys were county employees. He only had the support of one other county supervisor, John MacDonald, who also opposed the plan to contract with an outside nonprofit, and after the board voted in January 1988, Williams appeared to have lost this battle.

Amazingly, the board's nonprofit corporation deal began to unravel almost as soon as it was approved.

The estimated cost of starting up the Community Defender's system continued to rise. According to a report from Assistant County Administrative Officer David Janssen, the nonprofit program was going to cost more than a Public Defender's Office within county government. At that point, Supervisor Brian Bilbray changed his vote, saying the nonprofit was not going to be cost-effective. Now, with three votes on his side – a majority – Williams could help reverse course. Only a few months after the Community Defenders nonprofit won approval, the board voted 3-2 to revoke the nonprofit's contract.[16] The board then created a full-scale Public

Defender's Office within county government, just as Williams had advocated. His patience had paid off.

PROTECTING MOTORISTS FROM BAD SAMARITANS

In January, 1985, a legal secretary reported a horrifying story. Her car broke down on Interstate 5, near a downtown San Diego off-ramp. For the next four hours, cars streamed past her, including law enforcement vehicles. Finally, a man stopped and offered to drive her to a telephone. She accepted – only to have the false Samaritan pull a gun on her, drive to a remote road, and rape her.

The public was outraged, and so was Supervisor Leon Williams. He searched for a solution and remembered that he had seen emergency call boxes along some roads in the Los Angeles area. He thought that approach could work in San Diego, ensuring that stranded motorists no longer would fall prey to dangerous strangers. Ultimately the call boxes would pop up along highways all over the state. The legislation, introduced by state Sen. William Craven, a Republican from Oceanside, enabled any California county to create a Service Authority for Freeway Emergencies (SAFE) to install and manage a network of freeway call boxes. The system would be financed through an annual $1 fee on vehicle registrations.

In San Diego County, Williams, the fervent call box advocate, was the natural choice to become the SAFE chairman, helping to resolve contract and patent disputes before successfully overseeing the installation of the yellow solar-powered call boxes topped with blue highway signs. The first of them began operating in late 1988. By 1994, with Williams still serving as SAFE chairman, San Diego County had 1,350 call boxes along its freeways, with another 300 in the pipeline for segments of several state routes. The system helped thousands of stranded motorists with major emergencies or lesser problems ranging from overheated engines and empty gas tanks to flat tires. The public appreciated the service. "People are pleased with the convenience – the boxes are right there when needed and easy to use," said Colleen Carnevale, Williams's legislative assistant.[17] Eventually, cell phones reduced the need for call boxes, although they still come in handy for many motorists. But, thanks to Leon Williams, the call boxes on San Diego's freeways remain a symbol of government with a heart.

SHINING A LIGHT ON HATE

San Diego County – highly diverse and located on the U.S.-Mexico border – did not have a Human Relations Commission when Williams took his seat on the Board of Supervisors. The board had abolished an existing one in 1978, ostensibly to save money. But Williams thought that was a false economy. He believed there were plenty of reasons to reconstitute the commission. This was a county, after all, that had seen David Duke, the national Ku Klux Klan leader, ride into town vowing to keep Mexicans from crossing the border. At the north end of the county, Tom Metzger headed the White Aryan Resistance. There were also incidents of violence and discrimination reported against African Americans, gays and lesbians, Hispanics, and a growing population of Filipinos and other Asians, including a large influx of Vietnamese, Cambodian, Laotian and Hmong refugees after the Vietnam War. He thought a Human Relations Commission would give people a place to voice their complaints and provide education to help reduce bigotry.

Williams's longtime staffer, Neil Good, was especially eager to resurrect the Human Relations Commission. Good was active on many fronts. He was a journalist, a leader in the San Diego Democratic Party, and an advocate for the poor and homeless. Then, he revealed that he was about to pursue a new cause—gay activism. "He asked to talk to me in my office, and he went on talking and talking," recalled Williams. "Finally, he said, 'Leon, I'm trying to tell you I'm gay.'"[18]

Williams was caught by surprise because he knew Good was raising a daughter. Until then, Williams had not known that his aide was gay, although in characteristic fashion, it didn't make a bit of difference to Williams. In fact, it made sense for Good to come out. With so many gay men suffering from AIDS – and with public prejudice isolating very sick people – an advocate like Neil Good could not remain in the shadows. In 1987, Good ran for a seat on San Diego City Council seat. He made a strong showing but did not win. Two years later, Williams learned that his smart, energetic former assistant had fallen gravely ill. Shortly after, Good died from complications of hepatitis. He was 41. Williams thought that Good's death was a tragic loss for the entire community.

In his days on Williams's staff, Good had provided indispensable help in reviving the county's Human Relations Commission, despite the hesitancy of the more conservative board members. He announced Williams's proposal for the new county commission at a state Fair Employment and Housing Commission (FEHC) hearing on racial tensions. The state commissioners were skeptical. FEHC Commissioner Susan Weiner told Good, "It appears that other supervisors might not support your supervisor."[19]

Yet Williams fearlessly continued his campaign. In 1985, it was his turn to serve as Board of Supervisors chairman, a leadership position rotated among the supervisors, and during his State of the County speech, he made creation of the Human Relations Commission a priority. That year, Williams was able to win board approval to establish the commission. However, the new entity had little power. The staff for the 15-member commission was limited to a director and a secretary, and the commission was not granted investigative powers. "I had to accept what I could get through the board," explained Williams.[20]

His board colleagues also insisted that the commission refrain from investigating complaints from the gay community, largely due to the concerns of fundamentalist Christians. Their objections forced Williams to refashion a general mission statement for the commission. The new statement did not specify which groups could register their complaints with the commission. Nevertheless, Williams made sure that gay citizens – especially those with AIDS – had a sympathetic representative on the panel. One of Williams's original appointees to the commission was Dr. Brad Truax, a Hillcrest doctor serving the gay community and an advocate for AIDS anti-discrimination laws. Truax was the founder of San Diego Physicians for Human Rights and chairman of the regional Task Force on AIDS.

Despite its restrictions and limited staff, the new County Human Relations Commission found ways to focus attention on racial and ethnic issues and problems.

In 1988, at Williams's urging, the commission created a hate crimes registry, providing a central repository for the sheriffs' and police reports on crimes or offensive behavior that appeared to be linked to race, religion, sexual orientation, age, or disability.

The reports of the hate crimes registry showed that prejudice was alive and well in the county. From September 1990 through August 1991, the registry received 219 hate-crime reports, with the commission disclosing that more than half could be verified as hate crimes. The gay community, hit hard by the deadly AIDs epidemic, also endured the psychological sting of discrimination. Of the 116 verified hate-crime reports, 48 were based on sexual orientation. Another 45 incidents were racially related, including 20 against African Americans and 16 in which the victims were white. [21]

Williams often wished that the commission could play a larger role. In 1992, the police beating of Rodney King in Los Angeles and the ensuing riots signaled another racial crisis. Williams wistfully told a reporter, "After the Rodney King incidents, I would have liked the commission to call meetings, talk to the press, present public service announcements, help solve some of the problems. ... But it takes staff for that."[22]

The following year, even the commission's small staff disappeared. Despite Williams's objections, a majority of the county supervisors cut the commission's entire $100,000 funding, citing budget constraints. For the second time, the county government was left without a Human Relations Commission.

Nevertheless, the concept had caught on in the city of San Diego, which started its own Human Relations Commission in

1991. In the time that the county's commission operated, it had offered a forum for dialogue and appreciation for San Diego's multicultural population. And it had demonstrated that much still needed to be done to bring tolerance and harmony to San Diego County.

Leon Williams on the cover of the San Diego Metropolitan (2001)
Used courtesy of San Diego Metro Magazine

CHAPTER 9

Getting it Done – From Vision to Fruition

Leon Williams would be the first to say that holding public office can be a humbling experience. That's especially true when an official like Williams has definite ideas for improving the city and all of its neighborhoods. He can devise a series of plans and proposals, but he has to persuade others to hop on that bandwagon – or nothing will come of his glorious concepts.

The art of politics is all about finding the golden key to consensus. It means learning what motivates your colleagues, what moves them. It also means finding that common ground where a political figure can sow the seeds of compromise. Williams exercises those skills with an absence of confrontation. "I don't want to fight with anybody," he says. "I just want to do as much good as possible."

For Williams, the challenges started from Day One on the council. At that time, council inertia threatened his ambitious goals. In the late 1960s, his colleagues seemed in no particular hurry to take bold actions. Then there was partisan politics. Although city elections were officially nonpartisan, Williams's liberal Democratic social views were anathema to some of the council's Republicans. He recalled how one day, following a meeting, Councilman Lee Hubbard, the conservative owner of a concrete company, turned to Williams and bluntly told him, "I hate everything you stand for." Williams didn't respond with anger or hurtful words. He simply didn't give up on anyone.

For the most part, Williams could reason with his colleagues. They had their own ideas, but these ideas weren't necessarily set in stone. Keeping that in mind, Williams conditioned himself to listen to the others respectfully, without prejudice. They had his attention. He was careful never to level personal criticism against any of them. "I think criticizing people or trying to win an argument is doomed to fail in terms of changing somebody's mind or getting cooperation," he said.

But if colleagues mistook his polite manners for weakness, they quickly discovered how wrong they were. Williams would wait his turn to speak, and, in his calm voice, present his own proposals with conviction. Many resulted in approvals for projects and policies that he viewed as being in the best public interest.

Over his years of public service on elected and appointed boards and councils, Williams was able to develop effective strategies for advancing his positions. He would clearly state reasons for supporting a given measure. If his colleagues disagreed and seemed inclined to vote no, he found ways to help them see things differently. Here are some examples of his approach:

WHAT DO WE HAVE TO LOSE?

Occasionally, the City Council majority seemed predisposed to vote against a project without a strong reason. Opposing arguments seemed shapeless and ill-defined. Yet, this negative outlook could metastasize and doom a project. Williams found this psychological phenomenon puzzling and especially frustrating if he thought a proposal was particularly important for the community.

In one case, the fate of downtown redevelopment seemed to hang in the balance. The problem arose when the city of San Diego was in the planning stages for Horton Plaza shopping center downtown. Construction of a new parking garage was part of the deal, and the city gave its developer Ernest Hahn a deadline for coming up with financing. As the deadline approached, Hahn admitted that he didn't have his funding lined up yet, and he requested a deadline extension. Williams was horrified when he saw that some of his colleagues wanted to vote against Hahn's request. He thought of the consequences, the possibility that the entire Horton Plaza endeavor might implode. The shopping center and its garage were the commercial linchpins for redevelopment. Without them, who knew what other key elements would fade away? Williams also understood that a colleague or two who opposed Hahn's request really didn't care if downtown renewal failed.

When the matter came before the City Council, which made decisions as the city's Redevelopment Agency, Williams came up with an argument that resonated. What could the city lose by giving Hahn more time to meet his contractual obligations? "We would just lose time," said Williams. "We had nobody else to continue the project, and there was a chance of getting something positive out of it."

In the end, the council gave Hahn the time he needed, and the city was eventually rewarded with a stunning new downtown shopping complex and a parking garage that helped draw suburbanites back to the Centre City.

Another example of Williams's successful persuasion came with Kaiser Permanente's proposal to build a new hospital in the Grantville neighborhood near the east end of Mission Valley. Allen Hitch, the city councilman representing the area, opposed its construction. Williams thought his colleague exaggerated the negatives of the hospital and completely overlooked the advantages it might have. He pointed out that the hospital probably would not have the severe traffic impacts on the residential communities nearby that some people feared. The hospital site was on the fringe of Allied Gardens, accessible by already busy commercial streets, Friars and Mission Gorge. It also was close to freeways. The disruptions from construction would be temporary. And the resulting hospital would provide quality medical care for Kaiser Permanente members in the surrounding neighborhoods. "I thought it was an excellent site," said Williams. "I kept asking Allen Hitch, 'What possible harm could come from building this hospital at that location?'" Eventually, Hitch conceded, and a council majority, including Hitch, approved the project. Its construction made a major Kaiser facility available to San Diegans.

REFRAME ARGUMENTS

Williams always looked for a way to influence opinion without confrontation. People don't like to be told they're wrong, he knew, and they usually dig in their heels when they hear those words. When Williams disagreed with a proposal or wanted to win council approval for his position, he often did so by reframing an issue. He would paint a bigger picture for his colleagues by presenting previously unknown facts from a credible source, or by planting images in their minds that could expand their view. The goal was to let them reconsider an issue on their own terms, so that they could reach a different conclusion without feeling pressured.

On the Board of Supervisors, with a conservative majority not always enthusiastic about voting for social programs, Williams would make the case that some services deserve approval because they save the county tax dollars in the long run. Williams successfully convinced his fellow supervisors that prenatal care would be an investment in saving large amounts of taxpayers' dollars for the care of premature babies and infants with birth defects. And it would result in fewer low birth weight babies needing intensive care. He helped his colleagues consider aspects that some had not thought about before. In doing so, they joined him in doing the right thing.

Williams had a remarkable ability to make a positive out of something others thought was negative. For instance, during his tenure on the City Council, some council members disliked the fact that, at that time, they were nominated in their districts but had to run citywide in the general election. The fear was that distant voters who knew nothing about the candidate or the district could determine the outcome. And a bigger electorate could mean higher campaign expenses. After Williams left the council, this electoral system was changed so candidates ran only in their districts for both the primary and general election.

However, Williams did not mind running citywide. In fact, he found a way to turn the process around to his advantage. After all, under the citywide system, voters in his Fourth District also cast ballots for candidates in other parts of the city. If he wanted to persuade a council colleague to support a measure needed in his Fourth District, he would sometimes research the number of ballots his Fourth District voters cast for his fellow council member. In one case, he discovered that the number of votes a council colleague received from Fourth District voters exceeded the council member's margin of victory. So why not support the Fourth District people who helped deliver the win?

Sometimes Williams could alter a political conversation by changing the visual or emotional tenor of the discussion. He remembers a time during the Vietnam War when the San Diego Police Department came before the City Council with a proposal to ban military personnel from visiting San Diego's peep shows. The officer making the presentation described peep shows as dirty, immoral, and corrupting. In his quiet voice, Williams countered with a description of the horrific wartime conditions soldiers had experienced in Vietnam. "I told them that these returning soldiers had seen naked bodies in the war, dead and mutilated bodies, naked bodies burning from napalm. Surely, they could handle the sight of a naked woman at a peep show. The officer at the podium picked up his papers and said they would go back and work on it. And that was the last I saw of that proposal."

KNOW YOUR ALLIES

Lining up supporters for a particular cause can help smooth the path to approval, and Williams was a master of consensus building. He knew how to articulate the goal and figure out who could help. For instance, he had natural allies in the battle to ban smoking—medical experts and groups ranging from the American Lung Association to the American Cancer Society.

He also knew how to locate and communicate with sympathetic officials in other agencies. For instance, when Ronald Reagan was California governor, the state Highway Commission seemed determined to build Highway 252 project through Southcrest despite the community's unhappiness. The turning point came after Jerry Brown took over as California's Democratic governor in January 1975. The change in administrations gave Williams more access. A few years earlier, he had worked on Brown's campaign for California's secretary of state. As governor, Brown named San Diego Democrat Lynn Schenk as his secretary of business, transportation and housing. The new leadership listened to the request of the councilman and the people of Southcrest– and the state delivered. The freeway plan was stopped.

PACK THE HOUSE

Networking needs to happen at the grassroots, and Williams worked to mobilize his constituents to stand up for their own interests. One of his strategies was to organize town councils. Their members could show up and express their minds at City Council meetings. For example, opponents of Highway 252 packed the council chamber whenever that issue appeared on the council agenda, and many traveled long distances to attend California Highway Commission meetings.

TELL THE TRUTH

People don't always place truth and politics in the same sentence. But Williams believed that honesty works better in the long run. It's one thing to put your own spin on a particular issue to gain support. But it's quite another to promise voters something that an elected official could never hope to deliver. Williams used to cite the adage about the difference between a politician and a statesman. "A politician tells people what they want to hear," he would say. "A statesman tells them what they need to hear."

Please Be Reasonable

Sometimes rumors, fueled by emotion, swept through a community and threatened to undermine important public projects before they reached the decision makers. Williams learned the importance of coming to meetings prepared to respond with facts. He had to be ready to face a crowd of angry or confused people. They often wanted to know how they would be affected by a new city project. They wanted to vent their worst fears. And they deserved clear answers, especially if the rumors were wrong.

Such was the case when Williams, as chair of the Metropolitan Transit Development Board, was considering construction of a light-rail trolley line slated to run alongside Interstate 8. It was a segment of track deemed vital to a network serving the East County. Yet some residents near its proposed route north of San Diego State University did not agree. A group of them showed up at a board meeting, insisting the project would cause intolerable noise levels. Recalled Williams, "I remember one man stood up and said, 'That's going to be noisy.'"

Williams challenged the group to look at the project another way. The light rail actually might make their neighborhood a little quieter. "The trolley is going to make a lot less noise than automobiles," he told them. "A trolley with 500 people makes less noise than one motorcycle on the freeway. And this will take a lot of traffic off the highway. "

The opposition melted away, Williams said, adding that perhaps these citizens realized that they had been unreasonable.

TRY, TRY AGAIN

Elected and appointed officials rarely win every single proposal they advance or support. Williams was no exception. Yet even if he felt sure he was right about a defeated measure, he refused to show anger or frustration. From his years of experience, he understood the proposal may come up again, giving him a second chance to make his case. Sometimes the case made itself.

That is what happened when his colleagues on the transit agency board decided to save money by eliminating air conditioning on the trolley cars they were ordering for the light-rail line. Williams argued in vain that trolley cars sweltering in the hot months would turn off customers. The trolley would probably lose fare revenues as a result, wiping out any savings by going without air conditioning. But Williams was outvoted. Soon after the low-budget trolley cars went into service, the weather heated up – and the passengers' complaints rolled in. Ultimately, the trolley cars were retrofitted with air conditioning. Williams had the last word. "I told you so."

Leon Williams in his home (2011)
Image used courtesy of U-T

Chapter 10

Revisiting the City – Then and Now

March 20, 2014

Barbara Harris, better known as Sister Pee Wee, is sitting behind the red formica lunch counter when Leon Williams enters her little restaurant near the corner of 30th Street and Imperial Avenue.

Williams hasn't talked to her for a while, and he isn't certain she recognizes him. But the glance she gives him shows that she does. It's a look Williams frequently gets as he travels about his onetime council district – a slight smile or a nod to one of their beloved leaders. That is not surprising. As a neighbor, he had walked among them since World War II days. As a public figure, he had served them since 1969.

The sign from Sister Pee Wee's (1969)

Sister Pee Wee, 79, looks ageless. From this small establishment, which is celebrating its 50th anniversary, she has earned a spot on San Diego's culinary map with her fried chicken, pork chops, meatloaf, catfish, greens, and yams—her soul food.

Forty-five years earlier, Williams brought KPBS reporter Peter Kaye to this very same restaurant. The local public broadcasting station had been shooting a televised interview, profiling the new city councilman and his Fourth District. Williams highlighted Sister Pee Wee's Soul Food Restaurant as an example of the black-owned businesses flourishing in the district at the time.

From the KPBS interview with Barbara Harris (1969)
Image used courtesy of KPBS

Despite the passing years and a shift in neighborhood demographics from predominantly black to Latino, she is still behind her counter, serving her customers. Like a rock in a stream, Sister Pee Wee has survived the changes flowing around San Diego.

Williams's visit to Sister Pee Wee's restaurant is one stop along the route of his 1969 televised tour, when he drove the reporter from one end of the district to the other in his Ford Falcon. This time, he takes the wheel to revisit these streets. The goal is to note the changes, for better and worse, and the neighborhoods that still need official nurturing.

We start downtown on the top deck of the city's parking garage, the Parkade, where 45 years earlier, Williams and the KPBS reporter began their journey. The Parkade overlooks the same City Hall where Williams had first dreamed of renewing the Centre City and set out to help persuade power brokers that the fading downtown could - and should — be revived. And with Mayor Pete Wilson in the urban renewal camp, plans had been devised in the 1970s, a redevelopment agency energized and activated, and public funds identified for the enormous task ahead of them. The memories of those intense City Council debates — the long discussions over how to overcome roadblocks and the arm-twisting—still echo through the halls of a building that was itself a downtown renewal project in the 1960s.

The fruit of those efforts spread out all around our vantage point on the roof of the garage, a powerful example of how Williams, along with civic leaders, city planners, developers, investors, and a majority of the city's elected officials, united to save - and improve - a Centre City.

Beyond the City Hall complex and a few older office buildings nearby, downtown San Diego bears little resemblance to the city Williams toured in 1969. The growth is phenomenal. The downtown is dense with gleaming high-rises and restored and polished architectural gems. Williams nods approvingly at the signs of new construction all around, especially on the east side of downtown. "I always said the city bird should be the crane," he says, with a chuckle.

As we leave downtown and head south and then east, we pass the central library completed in 2013, the metal lattice of its dome gleaming in the noon sun. One side of the dome appears slightly unfinished, a deliberate and fitting architectural symbol showing that San Diego is still a work in progress.

Williams turns his SUV toward the lower-income, racially diverse neighborhoods beyond the East Village. We are going to visit the bright spots of renewal in neighborhoods too often starved of resources. But on this sight-seeing tour, Williams also wants to revisit problem areas that troubled him in 1969, some of which stubbornly persist to this day.

We move on to the eastern fringe of downtown, then pass through the neighborhoods of Barrio Logan, Sherman Heights, and Grant Hill, among others. In the years of segregation and restrictive racial covenants, some of these neighborhoods were the only ones where San Diego's African Americans could settle. Williams owned one of those homes years ago, and he points it out as we drive down Ocean View Boulevard. The little bungalow has been remodeled, but the driveway is still the same. "I made that driveway myself," he says.

On National Avenue, he arrives at another moment of nostalgia. He points out the Bank of America branch that gave him a loan in 1947 to buy a house in Golden Hill – and ignored race restrictions on the deed of the house.

We drive along street after street of bungalows, historic homes, apartments, and corner convenience stores – areas that benefitted from the years Williams spent representing their residents and business owners, ensuring the city would not let the roads and other infrastructure get less than their fair share of city resources. With his ceaseless desire to have more for the community, he is concerned that the economy of the area has not changed nearly enough since white residents migrated to the suburbs in the 1950s and 1960s. Williams's ideal for Southeastern San Diego, he explains, would restore a better socioeconomic balance, with a healthy mix of middle class and low-income residents to bring in more tax revenues and consumer spending.

Yet, along the major thoroughfares, the neighborhoods of Southeastern San Diego show signs of renewal. There are chain stores in areas previously starved for major supermarkets and consumer shopping. On Market Street, which rolls over a series of gentle hills like a children's rollercoaster, we pass Gateway Center. At one time, the city of San Diego owned the land and reserved it for cemetery uses. Williams supported a city ballot measure that removed some of the cemetery land for commercial development. Now, Gateway Center has a popular Costco warehouse store and an industrial park.

And along the Imperial Avenue corridor are developments bringing in amenities and needed services to neighboring residents. At 21st Street and Imperial Avenue is a neighborhood Wal-Mart, its lot so filled with customers' cars that we can't find a place to park. As we head east, Williams points to the beautiful Spanish-style police substation at 25th and Imperial. Just beyond the intersection at 40th Street we make a right turn into the busy parking lot of Imperial Marketplace, anchored by a Home Depot. Several restaurants and shops operate in the complex.

Turning onto Euclid Avenue, we stop at the King-Chavez Health Clinic, which opened in 2012 in a new 25,000-square foot building. Operated by the San Ysidro Health Center, it provides much-needed health and dental services to the surrounding neighborhoods. Williams – ever health-conscious – finds it appropriate that the clinic is on a site previously occupied by a fast-food restaurant.

The clinic's security guard at the entrance instantly recognizes Williams and points him to a plaque on the wall. It declares the huge waiting room on the lower floor of the clinic to be the Leon Williams Lobby, complete with a large, cheerful photo of the lobby's namesake. It is another of the many tokens of appreciation scattered throughout the community.

Afterwards, we drive to the Southcrest neighborhood along 43rd Street, looking for the urban renewal projects that replaced the 1.8-mile, weed and trash-strewn highway corridor left after the construction plan was dropped. As a councilman, Williams played a key leadership role in halting state Highway 252, which would have connected Interstates 805 and 5. Later, the Southeast Economic Development Corp. – the city renewal group created at Williams's behest – oversaw development of the land abandoned by Caltrans.

On this tour, we have to search a few minutes to find the exact borders of the former battleground. After years of constructing a shopping center, homes, and parks in the Southcrest neighborhood, the new and old sections of the neighborhood blend seamlessly. The nasty scar that state transportation officials inflicted across the community has been covered over and healed. At the heart of the old highway corridor is the Southcrest Plaza shopping center, site of a Gonzalez Northgate Market. This supermarket replaced Albertson's grocery store, which in its previous incarnation as Lucky's, had been the first chain supermarket in the area in 25 years. These days, shoppers go about their business peacefully, perhaps unaware of the fierce struggle that enabled them to have a supermarket instead of a freeway.

We pass a cluster of large, modern homes with well-kept yards, similar to the kind found in the north city suburbs. Former SEDC director Reese Jarrett used to make light of Williams's insistence on building some of these single-family dwellings as part of redevelopment scheme. To Williams, this wasn't really a laughing matter. He wanted something for middle-class homebuyers in SEDC's territory, not just dense housing "projects" for the poor. "Reese used to call one of the models in this subdivision the Leon Williams model," notes Williams, smiling.

We circle back toward downtown to survey one of Williams's biggest disappointments – the continued existence of dirty, polluting businesses cheek to jowl with single-family homes along Commercial Street. "The people have to wake up every day and look at that ugliness, and they feel helpless to do anything about it," he remarks. We come to an auto graveyard at Commercial and 32nd Street – the same business he pointed out to the KPBS reporter on the original tour. "It's still here," he observes.

The whole intent of zoning in the first place was to separate residential and industrial uses. In order to let businesses set up shop, the city had granted them spot zoning and variances. Williams said he would have opposed those zoning exceptions if he had a chance, but the decisions were often made by bureaucrats and never reached the City Council. He felt that spot zoning like this would never be accepted in the newer, predominantly white middle-class residential subdivisions. Once these businesses had the city's permission, they stuck like burrs to this urban neighborhood. "I told them this would happen," said Williams, who noted that his warnings and predictions came true. Of course, the dirty businesses create jobs and revenue, and I ask him where they should relocate. "Somewhere up north," he replies, sardonically.

Meanwhile, there is no indication that either the businesses or residents plan to move out, meaning that land use will continue to be a struggle. On June 3, 2014, San Diego voters rejected a City Council-approved community plan for Barrio Logan. It would have created a buffer zone between heavy industry and homes—a plan long desired by barrio residents. Shipyards around the barrio led the opposition campaign, arguing the plan could hurt their businesses and their suppliers.

We move along Commercial Street next to the San Diego Trolley's Orange Line tracks. Williams hopes that one day the trolley stations will serve as a magnet for residential development. As we cruise down the street, he looks sadly at the old warehouses, junkyards, and recycling centers that still proliferate along the route.

Then I spot construction activity just north of 25th and Commercial in Logan Heights and point it out to Williams. A few steps from the 25th Street trolley station, workers are hammering together the frame of a sprawling new apartment complex, with 130 affordable units and 70 units for seniors. Construction of this massive structure overshadows the low industrial buildings hunkered down along Commercial. New housing is staking its claim along the trolley line. And once completed, its residents will be able to step onto a public transit system that can deliver them to key points of the community, whether it is downtown or Old Town, the grocery store or the department stores in Mission Valley. The housing complex on the trolley line is one sign that the seeds of change sown many years earlier are still taking root here.

Williams knows, however, that improving a city is a task that never ends. There will always be the need for yet another project, whether it's expanding a sewage treatment plant, eliminating blight, modernizing the urban infrastructure, or enacting policies to create more jobs. There may be many ways to reach those shared goals, and not everyone will agree on which path to take. City officials will have to make it happen and convince the public that their leaders are headed in the right direction. Williams understands that progress takes more than good intentions. And he offers advice that worked well during his long career. Use the tools of rational argument, respect, and consensus. Wield them deftly – and with a smile. And above all, use them to build and then reinvent a welcoming and inclusive city.

Acknowledgments

This book owes its existence to the dozens of interviews that Leon Williams generously provided over the course of two years. His devoted wife, Margaret, deserves special thanks. Her help was indispensable in locating photos and documents. Her encouragement and her profound faith in the significance of his story kept the book on track.

The book benefitted from the wise guidance of Kim Mazyck, publishing manager at Montezuma Publishing, and the copy editing and book design skills of Stephanie Lauridsen. Also, many friends, former staff members, and supporters of Leon Williams contributed information, among them William Jones, Wes Pratt, Vernon Sukumu, Arlene Kirsch, Janice Graham Heather, and Colleen Carnavale. Thanks also go to journalist Gary Shaw, who conducted the initial interviews and provided helpful assistance along the way. Carlos LeGerrette took the dramatic photo of Leon Williams against the backdrop of the magnificent city.

The book would not have been the same without the help and keen insight of Tom Larwin, former general manager of the Metropolitan Transit Development Board. Rob Schupp, at the San

Diego Metropolitan Transit System, was quick to answer my queries, including a study produced 20 years earlier. Longtime city planner and redevelopment expert Max Schmidt also provided details from the beginnings of a grand era in San Diego history.

Notes

Introduction

1. William Jones (former Williams's staff aide, former city councilman), interview with the author, June 20, 2014.

2. Daniel M. Weintraub, "Williams' Quiet, Political Artistry Builds Solid, Satisfied Constituency," *Los Angeles Times*, November 30, 1986, San Diego Edition, Metro 2.

3. Leon Williams, interview with author, April 29, 2013.

4. "17 Mile Drive Public Use Agreement," October 20, 1987, accessed March 10, 2015, http://www.co.monterey.ca.us/planning/docs/plans/17%20Mile%20Drive%20Public%20Use%20Agreement%2010-20-1987.pdf.

5. Leon Williams, interview with the author, November 7, 2013.

6. Arlene Kirsch (former legal and press aide to County Supervisor Leon Williams), interview with the author, October 29, 2014.

7. "Guide to the Alpha Pi Boule Records 1965/2003," Online Archives of California, Contributed by San Diego State University, http://www.oac.cdlib.org/search?style=oac4&ff=0&query=Alpha+Pi+Boul%C3%A9+Records&x=13&y=13.

8. "The Way It Was: Alumni Diversity Award Winner Reflects on His Campus Experience," SDSU Alumni enewsletter, accessed October 7, 2014, http://www.sdsualumni.org/s/997/index2.aspx?pgid=1319&gid=1.

CHAPTER ONE

1. Leon Williams, interview with the author, April 10, 2013.

2. Leon Williams, phone interview with the author, January 19, 2015.

3. Leon Williams, interview with the author, March 23, 2013.

4. Leon Williams, interview with the author, July 16, 2014.

5. "Tulsa Race Riot," *Oklahoma History Society's Encyclopedia of History and Culture*, accessed October 7, 2013, http://digital. library.okstate.edu/ENCYCLOPEDIA/ENTRIES/T/TU013.ht ml.

6. "History of Langston University," Langston University, accessed October 7, 2014, http://www.langston.edu/about-us/resources/history-langston-university.

7. Leon Williams, interview with the author, April 6, 2013.

8. Ibid.

9. Adrian Florido, "One of San Diego's Black Pioneers," *Voice of San Diego*, April 8, 2011, http://voiceofsandiego.org/2011/04 /08one-of-san-diegos-black-pioneers.

10. Robert Fikes, Jr., "The Black in Crimson and Black: a History and Profiles of African Americans at San Diego State University," 2013, accessed January 12, 2015, https://adminlb.imodules.com.

CHAPTER TWO

1. Leon Williams, interview with Peter Kaye (KPBS San Diego), March 1, 1969.

2. Vernon Sukumu, phone interview with the author, March 20, 2015.

3. "Leon Williams Takes Oath as Councilman," *San Diego Union*, January 8, 1969, B-1.

4. William Jones (former Williams's staff aide, former city councilman), interview with the author, June 20, 2014.

5. Leon Williams, interview with the author, August 30, 2013.

6. Ibid.

7. Leon Williams, interview with the author, September 19, 2014.

8. Williams, interview with the author, August 5, 2013.

9. Ibid.

10. Ibid.

11. San Diego City Council, "An Ordinance Establishing a Schedule of Compensation for the Mayor and Members of the City Council of the City of San Diego for the Period July 1, 1978 through June 30, 1980." May 16, 1978, http://docs.sandiego.gov/council_reso_ordinance/rao2014/R-308800.pdf.

12. William Jones, interview with the author, June 20, 2014.

13. The controversy over council pay continued through 2015, with San Diego council members continuing to be paid far less than county supervisors, whose salaries were tied to judicial pay. "Pay Raises for City Council? Bring in the Judge," *U-T San Diego*, March 8, 2015, Section Main News.

14. William Jones, interview with the author, June 20, 2014.

15. Leon Williams, interview with the author, June 20, 2014.

16. William Jones, interview with the author, June 20, 2014.

17. Ibid.

18. Ibid.

19. Wes Pratt (former Williams's staff aide, former city councilman), interview with the author, March 4, 2015.

20. Barry Horstman, "Judge Orders That Pratt Be Given Place on Council Ballot," *Los Angeles Times*, August 15, 1987.

21. Wes Pratt, e-mail to the author, March 4, 2015.

CHAPTER THREE

1. "Hoover Warns of New Left," UPI, *San Diego Union*, January 1, 1969.

2. "Citizens Interracial Committee," San Diego State University Library & Information Access, accessed April 17, 2015, http://library.sdsu.edu/scua/citizens-interracial-committee.

3. Leon Williams, interview with the author, March 30, 2013.

4. Williams, interview with the author, August 14, 2014.

5. Williams, interview with the author, August, 5, 2013.

6. Williams, interview with the author, December 9, 2014.

7. Ibid.

8. Williams, interview with the author, January 5, 2015.

9. Ibid.

10. Vernon Sukumu, phone interview with the author, March 20, 2015.

11. "Issues in Panther, 'US' Strife Bared," *San Diego Union*, August 16, 1969, B-1.

12. Leon Williams, interview with the author, January 5, 2015.

13. Curtis J. Austin, *Up Against a Wall: Violence in the Making and Unmaking of the Black Panther Party* (Fayetteville: University of Arkansas Press, 2006), 232.

14. Ibid., 240.

15. Leon Williams, interview with the author, April 29, 2013.

16. Leon Williams, interview with the author, August 14, 2014.

17. Ibid.

18. Elizabeth Fitzsimmons, "Sagon Penn Found Dead in Apparent Suicide," *San Diego Union-Tribune*, July 5, 2002, http://legacy.utsandiego.com/news/metro/20020705-9999_1m5sagon.html.

19. James Grimaldi, "New Police Image Draws Fire," *(San Diego) Evening Tribune*, November 11, 1987, B-1.

20. Leon Williams, interview with the author, August 14, 2014.

CHAPTER FOUR

1. Campaign brochure for Leon Williams's primary race, Fourth District San Diego City Council, 1969.

2. Leon Williams, interview with the author, November 7, 2013.

3. "Election History – Council District 4, City of San Diego," accessed April 8, 2015, http://www.sandiego.gov/city-clerk/pdf/cd4results.pdf.

4. Ibid.

5. "Judge Tells Council to Redistrict," *San Diego Union*, April 9, 1971, B-1.

6. "Equity and Elections," *San Diego Union*, April 13, 1971, B-6.

7. Ernesto Flores, "Mexican-American Group Says City Attorney Biased," *San Diego Union*, Sept. 9, 1972, B-3.

8. Leon Williams, phone interview with the author, September 25, 2014.

9. "Landt Critical of Ethnic Mix in Redistricting," *San Diego Union*, January 17, 1973, B-3.

10. Leon Williams, interview with the author, September 19, 2014.

11. "Council Accepts Redistricting Plan at Court Deadline," *San Diego Union*, January 24, 1973, B-1.

12. Leon Williams, interview with the author, November 7, 2013.

Chapter Five

1. Leon Williams, interview with the author, April 29, 2013.

2. Ibid.

3. Frank Exharos, "Building Boom Puts Curb on City Programs," *San Diego Union*, B-1, January 10, 1969.

4. Leon Williams, interview with the author, September 19, 2014.

5. "San Diego City Council Resolution No. 215958," May 12, 1976, http://docs.sandiego.gov/council_reso_ordinance /rao1976/R-215958.pdf.

6. Leon Williams, interview with the author, April 29, 2013.

7. "Builder Sues City Over Subdivision," *San Diego Union*, December 2, 1971, B-1.

8. University Towne Center—City Council approval, "Resolution No. 213245: Planned Commercial Development Permit No. 2," May 8, 1975, http://docs.sandiego.gov/council_reso_ordinance /rao1975/R-213245.pdf.

9. Leon Williams, interview with the author, January 28, 2015.

10. William Jones, interview with the author, June 20, 2014.

11. Leon Williams, interview with the author, March 20, 2014.

12. Ibid.

13. Leon Williams, interview with the author, August 5, 2013.

14. Ibid.

15. "The Takeover of Chicano Park," The History of Chicano Park, accessed November 9, 2014, http://www.chicanoparksandiego .com/history/page1.html.

16. Leon Williams, interview with the author, August 30, 2013.

CHAPTER SIX

1. Leon Williams, interview with the author, August 30, 2013.

2. Margaret C. Berg, Dan Berger, and Peter Jensen, *San Diego: Where Tomorrow Begins* (Northridge: Windsor Publications, 1987), 54.

3. Ibid., 54.

4. Leon Williams, interview with the author, April 6, 2013.

5. Ibid.

6. Reiner M. Hof, "The Formative Years, 1958-63, the Redevelopment of Downtown San Diego," *The Journal of San Diego History* 36, no. 1 (Winter 1990).

7. Max Schmidt, phone interview with the author, December 3, 2014.

8. Community Redevelopment Law of the State of California was found in California Health and Safety Code, § 33000.

9. Max Schmidt, phone interview with the author, December 3, 2014.

10. Leon Williams, phone interview with the author, April 29, 2013.

11. Williams, interview with the author, October 9, 2013.

12. Ibid.

13. Ibid.

14. Donna L. Alm (Director of Marketing & Communication, Centre City Development Corp.), letter to Leon Williams, July 8, 1995. The letter invited Williams to receive a director's award at the CCDC board meeting July 21, 1995.

15. "Builder Urges a Downtown Sports Arena," *San Diego Union-Tribune*, August 1, 1992, B-8.

16. Leon Williams, interview with the author, August 30, 2013.

17. Ibid.

18. Max Schmidt, phone interview with the author, December 3, 2014.

19. Roger Showley and Lori Weisberg, "Downtown vs. Neighborhoods," *UT San Diego*, February 7, 2014, A-1.

Chapter Seven

1. "MTS Announces Record 95 Million Passengers Rode the Bus And Trolley ion FY 2014," press release, San Diego Metropolitan Transit System, August 19, 2014, http://www.sdmts.com/MTS/MTSAnnouncesaRecord95MillionPassengersRodetheBusandTrolleyinFY2014.asp.

2. Gail P., "Grantville Station," Yelp, March, 2011, accessed March 24, 2015, http://www.yelp.com/biz/grantville-trolley-station-san-diego.

3. Leon Williams, interview with the author, November 7, 2013.

4. Ibid.

5. Leon Williams and Tom Larwin, interview with the author, February 5, 2014.

6. Benjamin Shore, "Mid-Coast Trolley Funds Requested," Copley News Service, *San Diego Union*, April 27, 1990, B-3.

7. Joe Hughes, "UCSD Now Backing Campus Trolley Route," *(San Diego) Evening Tribune*, April 27, 1990, B-1.

8. Ibid.

9. Jeffrey Martin, "Blue Line Crime Study," San Diego Association of Governments at the request of Metropolitan Transit Development Board, 1994.

10. "Understanding Transit's Impact on Public Safety," San Diego Association of Governments, June 2009, http://sandiegohealth .org/sandag/publicationid_1483_10995.pdf.

11. Jay Schneider, "Big Tram on Campus," *Building Design & Construction*, March 19, 2007, 41.

12. "MTS Dedicates SDSU Trolley Station to Leon Williams," press release, San Diego Metropolitan Transit System, July 1, 2011, http://www.sdmts.com/MTS/SDSULeonWilliamsDedication. asp.

CHAPTER EIGHT

1. Cheryl Clark, "AIDS Panel Feels Ignored by the Board," *San Diego Union*, November 5, 1987, B-1.

2. Claude Walbert, "County Oks New Office to Oversee AIDS Fight," *(San Diego) Evening Tribune*, June 3, 1987, B-3.

3. Robert Meyers, "More Women Going Without Care in S.D. County," *San Diego Union*, October 23, 1988, A-12.

4. Thomas R. Moore et al., "The Perinatal and Economic Impact of Prenatal Care in a Low-Socioeconomic Population," *American Journal of Obstetrics & Gynecology*, 154 (January 1986): 29-33.

5. Ibid.

6. Robert Meyers, "More Women Going Without Care in S.D. County," *San Diego Union*, October 23, 1988, A-12.

7. Gene Yasuda, "Supervisor Calls for New Agency to Operate Jails," *Los Angeles Times*, January 17, 1990, 1.

8. Ruth McKinnie, "County Acts to Hike Availability of Care for Poor, Pregnant," *(San Diego) Evening Tribune*, November, 8, 1990, B-7.

9. Ruth McKinnie, "Aid Urged for Drug-Using Expectant Moms," *(San Diego) Evening Tribune*, April 25, 1990, B-2.

10. Eric Young, "Teen Parents Urge Peers to Think First," *San Diego Union-Tribune*, April 23, 1995, B-2.

11. Leon Williams, interview with the author, January 18, 2014.

12. "History of the Surgeon General's Reports on Smoking and Health," Centers for Disease Control and Prevention, accessed March 30, 2015, http://www.cdc.gov/tobacco/data_statistics /sgr/history/.

13. Carol Sottili, "County May Stiffen Law on Smoking," *San Diego Union*, April 6, 1988, B-1.

14. Debra Kelley (regional director, California, American Lung Association), phone interview with the author, March 26, 2014.

15. Leon Williams, interview with the author, January 18, 2014.

16. Claude Walbert, "County Rejects Contract with Defenders Group," *(San Diego) Evening Tribune*, May 17, 1988, A-1.

17. Joe Hughes, "Call-Box Network is being Expanded to Rural Highways," *San Diego Union-Tribune*, September 5, 1994, B-1.

18. Leon Williams, interview with the author, January 18, 2014.

19. Dan Weikel, "County Panel Proposed to Help Ease Race Tension," *San Diego Union*, November 9, 1984, B-1.

20. Angela Lau, "San Diego's Racial History: Failures to Achieve Harmony," *San Diego Union-Tribune*, July 12, 1992, B-1.

21. Mary Curran-Downey, "Hate Crimes Rise 28 % in 1 Year: Gays, Lesbians are No. 1 Target," *San Diego Union-Tribune*, May 6, 1992, B-1.

22. Angela Lau, "San Diego's Racial History: Failures to Achieve Harmony," *San Diego Union-Tribune*, July 12, 1992, B-1.

CHAPTER NINE

1. Leon Williams, interview with the author, August 30, 2013.

2. Williams, interview with the author, March 23, 2013.

3. Williams, interview with the author, August 30, 2013.

4. Williams, interview with the author, April 29, 2013.

5. Williams, interview with the author, April 6, 2013.

6. Williams, interview with the author, August 14, 2014.

7. Williams, interview with the author, June 20, 2014.

8. Williams, interview with the author, October 9, 2013.

INDEX

CPSIA information can be obtained at www.ICGtesting.com
Printed in the USA
LVOW02*0254240615

443611LV00006B/7/P